SPORTSPERFORMANCE
NAUTILUS.
BUILDING A HARD BODY

MICHAEL D. WOLF, Ph.D.

CONTEMPORARY
BOOKS, INC.
CHICAGO ■ NEW YORK

Library of Congress Cataloging-in-Publication Data

Wolf, Michael D.
  Nautilus: building a hard body.

  (Sportsperformance)
  1. Weight lifting.   2. Nautilus training.
I. Title.   II. Series.
GV546.W638   1987   613.7'1   87-6876
ISBN 0-8092-4772-0 (pbk.)

Copyright © 1987 by International Fitness Exchange
All rights reserved
Published by Contemporary Books, Inc.
180 North Michigan Avenue, Chicago, Illinois 60601
Manufactured in the United States of America
Library of Congress Catalog Card Number: 87-6876
International Standard Book Number: 0-8092-4772-0

Published simultaneously in Canada by Beaverbooks, Ltd.
195 Allstate Parkway, Valleywood Business Park
Markham, Ontario L3R 4T8 Canada

Portions of the "Interval Training" section in Chapter 4 are reprinted with permission from an article by the author that appeared in the October 1986 issue of *Home Gym & Fitness* magazine.

The section "Finding Quality in Commercial Fitness Centers" in Chapter 11 is reprinted with permission from an article by the author that appeared in the August 1986 issue of *Better Health & Living* magazine.

The section on "Home Fitness Equipment" in Chapter 11 is reprinted with permission from an article by Irving Dardik, M.D., and the author that appeared in the September/October 1985 issue of *Rx Being Well*.

All illustrations by Vanessa Hill.

Photo credits: Chapters 6–9, copyright Marti Cohen-Wolf; Chapter 11, courtesy of individually listed manufacturers; Chapter 12, courtesy of Nautilus Sports/Medical Industries, Inc.

CONTENTS

1	Introduction	1
2	Fitness and Nutrition: The Latest on Whom to Listen To and What's Being Said	5
3	The Science of Strength	19
4	Combining Strength and Aerobic Conditioning	27
5	Introduction to Nautilus Training	44
6	The Lower Body	58
7	The Abdomen and Lower Back	75
8	The Torso and Shoulders	82
9	The Arms	114
10	28—Count 'Em—28 Nautilus Workouts	129
11	Where to Work Out	142
12	The Latest from Nautilus	160
	Index	165

I'm grateful to the following people for their help in making this book happen: My wife and photographer Marti Ann Cohen-Wolf; Models Brenda Ingorgia, Jerry Conklin, Jan Stritzler, and Pam Coy; and Kyle Roggenbuck and Nancy Crossman of Contemporary Books.

1
INTRODUCTION

Here I sit, having written two quality books on Nautilus training, and knowing that other authors have also written books on the topic. I wonder why anyone should buy yet another Nautilus book. Or why they should choose this one over the others. The college-education fund for my year-old son, Evan, aside, I'd like to think that educated consumers will look over my work, hold it side by side with its competitors, and march right to the cashier. I want to take this chance to introduce you to the book and tell you why *this* is the book for you.

FITNESS AND NUTRITION: THE LATEST ON WHOM TO LISTEN TO AND WHAT THEY'RE SAYING

You'll learn what credentials to look for in those you plan to trust for exercise and nutritional guidance. After the lowdown on academic degrees and professional certifications, you'll get the late-breaking news on strength and aerobic training; updates on what, when, and how to eat to maintain a healthy body weight or reduce unwanted body fat; and details on the state of the art in body-composition measurement.

SPORTSPERFORMANCE

THE SCIENCE OF STRENGTH

After defining some basic terms, we'll delve into what the experts currently think about strength, endurance, power, and the training and equipment required to attain them.

COMBINING STRENGTH AND AEROBIC CONDITIONING

I am one of the world's strongest believers in balanced training, so you're going to get a truckload of information on aerobic conditioning in *this* Nautilus book. While muscular strength and power are fine goals, health, fitness, and quality athletic performance require true aerobic exercise.

You'll get (1) a detailed guide to aerobic training, with sections on how to write both a personalized exercise prescription and an interval-training prescription; (2) the lowdown on warming up, stretching, and cooling down; and (3) a complete set of instructions on how to best combine strength and aerobic training in your weekly schedule.

NAUTILUS TRAINING— INTRODUCTION

If you're looking for a treatise on company history and the life and times of founder and ex-owner Arthur Jones, or are expecting a 3-page promo on why no other equipment is as good as Nautilus, you're in the wrong place. This is a how-to book where you will learn what Nautilus is and why it works, what the training rules are, and what types of general workout strategies you can follow.

THE TRAINING CHAPTERS: LOWER BODY, ABDOMEN AND LOWER BACK, TORSO, AND ARMS

Through photos and clear text you'll learn how to properly use 25 Nautilus machines. This book is meant to

INTRODUCTION

be used at your local fitness center. Because so many of the Nautilus instructors you will come across are inadequately trained, both your safety and your results will be maximized if you pack the book in your gym bag.

NAUTILUS WORKOUTS

If you're dissatisfied with the workouts your local Nautilus staff members have prescribed for you, or if you're looking for some variety, you'll find a selection of time-proven Nautilus workouts here, including the use of negative-accentuated, negative-emphasized, and negative-only training.

WHERE TO WORK OUT

I'll offer my opinions on choosing a fitness center, maximizing the gains from your membership dollars, the results you can get from training on your own at home, and what to look for if you do decide to train at home.

THE LATEST FROM NAUTILUS

As we went to press, Nautilus unveiled their four new low-friction commercial machines: the Rotary Torso, Compound Rowing, Torso Arm, and Bench Press units. Hot-off-the-press photos and instructions will close the book.

It's my hope that you'll devote serious effort to reading and learning what I'm going to tell you. In the three years since my first Nautilus book was published, and after a great deal of thought, I still can't figure out why people will spend hundreds of dollars and hundreds of hours training on strength and aerobic equipment, yet not invest a few hours and dollars on a book that will maximize safety and effectiveness. Since you're reading this, you've taken the initial step. If you're in the bookstore, take out your wallet. (Buy copies for friends and relatives, too!) If you're at home, turn off the stereo, turn on a good reading light. Let's get started.

SPORTSPERFORMANCE

2
FITNESS AND NUTRITION: THE LATEST ON WHOM TO LISTEN TO AND WHAT'S BEING SAID

When you have a toothache, do you search from mouth to mouth looking for someone with perfect teeth to treat you, assuming that if their teeth are perfect they must be tooth experts? Of course not. You find the nearest dental professional.

When you've got a fever, do you run around sticking a thermometer in every mouth (or worse) you can find until you locate a 98.6 temperature, under the assumption that if their temperature is normal they must be temperature experts? Of course not. You look for a trained physician.

Then why on earth do about 95% of your contemporaries trust any female with Hollywood screen credits, big breasts, and tight buns, or any male with big pecs and big quads for guidance on health, fitness, and nutrition? Thank goodness that several years of uproar by the real experts have finally convinced many Hollywood gurus to consult experts before they write their books or release their videotapes. In general, though, so much damage has been done that volumes of books are needed to right the wrongs.

The American public needs to be convinced that exercise and nutrition are not areas one becomes expert in after working out for a few years, or reading *Eat To Win* (perish the thought). Those of us who worked long and hard to become trained exercise scientists shudder at the pseudo-science being peddled by some Hollywood star/starlet or trainer to the stars. My main goal is to give you the best and latest information in those areas that will have the greatest impact on the quality of your life and play: nutrition and exercise. In this chapter, I'll discuss who I think is worth listening to ("Credentials"), and what are the latest research results ("The News on Fitness" and "The News on Nutrition").

CREDENTIALS

I know as well as the next guy that letters after your name are no guarantee that you're an expert, or even good at what you claim to do. I see degrees and certifications as a type of insurance policy. The chances that someone with a college or graduate degree from a reputable institution, and/or professional certifications, will be worthy of your trust are greater than if you relied on someone with a mail-order degree or certificate.

FITNESS

In fitness, the minimum credential is a B.A. or B.S. in physical education. What this degree commonly includes is one course in the physiology of exercise, one course in the physics of movement (biomechanics), one course in testing and measurement, and possibly coursework in the psychology of exercise and motor learning (how to teach motor skills). A B.A. or B.S. gives you a good start in fitness, but it doesn't make you an expert.

An M.S. or M.A. degree in physical education involves in-depth coursework in one or more areas (such as exercise physiology). Many schools require a thesis research project, and offer or require internships. An exercise physiologist with a master's degree will most likely have sufficient training to assess your level of fitness, determine your specific needs, and write your "exercise prescription." Graduates of solid exercise physiology postbaccalaureate programs can usually be called true fitness professionals.

Doctoral studies in physical education can lead to either a Ph.D. (Doctor of Philosophy), an Ed.D. (Doctor of Education), or a P.E.D. (Doctor of Physical Education). In the matters important to you, there are few significant differences among the degrees. If any fitness professional can truly be called an exercise "expert," it's usually one who has spent three years beyond a master's degree earning a doctorate.

PROFESSIONAL CERTIFICATIONS

Though some universities now offer graduate degrees that specifically prepare students for careers in fitness (as opposed to research or teaching), many physical educators are pursuing professional certification to enhance their credentials. Clearly the national leader in certification of nondance fitness professionals is the American College of Sports Medicine (ACSM). Headquartered in Indianapolis, it has for more than four years been certifying fitness pros in rehabilitative exercise programs, and has recently begun certification programs in fitness for healthy persons. In assessing the fitness credentials of someone to whom you may entrust your body, an ACSM certification plus an undergrad or graduate degree can't be beat.

In the realm of aerobic dance certification, distinct from programs in general fitness administered by the ACSM, there are at least 20 organizations that offer a piece of parchment. The two biggest and most highly regarded are the Aerobics and Fitness Association of America (AFAA) and the International Dance Exercise Association (IDEA). Instructors possessing either certification are probably capable of choreographing a safe class, teaching it, and adapting it to the diverse skill and fitness levels of the participants. While there are other purveyors of aerobic certification, most experts advise that you look for IDEA or AFAA after an instructor's name.

NUTRITION

Much as in fitness, students wanting to become nutrition professionals can begin with a general B.A. or B.S. program, then develop deeper and broader expertise with a master's or doctoral studies. The certification to look for if you need an expert in dietary analysis and planning is R.D., or registered dietician. And though anyone can join, membership in the American Dietetics Association is a sign of interest in professional growth and camaraderie.

THE NEWS ON FITNESS

The news in strength is that you don't have to work as long as you thought to get strong, tight, or big. The news in aerobic exercise is that you don't have to work as hard as you thought. All in all, pretty exciting stuff for those of us who don't have three hours a day to devote to exercise. These items and others are discussed below.

STRENGTH TRAINING UPDATE

"Quality, not quantity" are the three key words in strength training if you're after fit, sculptured muscles. As you might know from my earlier Nautilus books, high-technology strength-training equipment has so focused intensity on your skeletal muscles that, if you follow the instructions in the pages to come, you'll need no more than one set of 12 to 15 repetitions for maximal strength gains. (Though, as we'll also get to, power training is somewhat different.)

Individual differences. Researchers are more appreciative than ever of the marked individual differences in response to training. There's an old (and appropriate) joke in which the professor stands up on the first day of class and says,

FITNESS AND NUTRITION

"Twenty percent of what I'm about to teach you is true. Unfortunately, I'm not sure which twenty percent." The advice that follows is guaranteed to work for some of you; unfortunately, I can't tell which of you. Our knowledge of the determinants of strength gain through weight training, and aerobic gain through aerobic training, is in its infancy. We do know there are powerful genetic limits on how fast, powerful, big, and strong we can be. We do know that some muscles will grow like weeds in response to one intense set of 12 repetitions, while others will get stronger but not change in size. The following chart lists my own training gains after nine months of intense, one-set, one-on-one training when I was research coordinator at Nautilus:

Muscle (Machine)	Pretraining		Posttraining	
	Size	Pounds	Size	Pounds
Chest (Double Chest)	40.5"	60	44.0"	110
Biceps (Multi-Biceps)	13.0"	50	13.5"	100
Quadriceps (Leg Extension)	21.0"	80	22.0"	160

See my point? Training with strict adherence to Nautilus guidelines (more on that later), and with probably the finest personal trainer to have ever worked on the equipment (Ken Hutchins), I doubled my strength on the Multi-Biceps and Leg Extension machines with negligible gains in muscular size, yet with the same strength increase, I put almost four inches on my chest (pectorals and latissimus). I have seen this not-so-phenomenal occurrence scores of times since my Nautilus-Florida days.

What can exercise science do for you, now that it is aware how individual each muscle's response is to a training stimulus? Not much, unfortunately. You can try other machines, or free weights, or calisthenics, on those stubborn muscles that won't grow, but if "strength without size" is in the genetic code for your biceps, as it must be for mine, you have to learn to live with it. One hidden benefit: people in the gym always stare in wonder and awe at how my unimpressive biceps can move so much weight!

Males and females. Our new investigations into the genetic and biochemical determinants of training gains have also yielded information on how men and women vary in response to exercise. Of most interest in a book on Nautilus training is, of course, the issue of size in women. Do women get big from Nautilus, or strength training in general?

Once again, the answer is "It depends." (Don't you love my expertise in technical writing?) While we recently thought that the amount of male sex hormones circulating in a woman's bloodstream determined how large her muscles would grow, current research suggests that this is not so. The answer may be genetically coded. As on my body, where some muscles respond with growth and strength, and some with just strength, some women may respond more "graphically" than others. How can you tell in advance which category you're in? You probably can't—only time and training will tell. But the odds are that few muscles on a woman's body will respond to strength training with both size and strength gains.

Cyclical training. Of more practical interest than information that tells you "It's out of your hands" is research into the need to periodically vary your workouts. The precise patterning of workout variation is called "cyclical training." Essentially, training gains have been found to plateau or stagnate if the same strength exercises are performed for more than 9 to 12 weeks. If you're a college or

FITNESS AND NUTRITION

professional athlete, your training cycles will correspond to key points in the season. If you're a nonathlete, and strength training simply for personal reasons, your best bet is to change exercises every two to three months. Since this requires your joining a fitness center that has more options than 12 basic Nautilus machines, I've included a chapter toward the back of the book that will help you select the right fitness center.

AEROBIC TRAINING UPDATE

Minimum required intensity. There's good news for those who thought that aerobic benefits (control of body weight, reduced risk of heart disease, etc.) required exercise that brought on heavy breathing, heavy sweating, and high heart rates. Recent research has shown that those who are unfit can derive noticeable aerobic benefit from exercise at as little as 55%–60% of their maximum, age-adjusted heart rate (HR). (To get an estimate of your maximum heart rate, subtract your age from 220.) For a 40-year-old, sedentary male, with an age-adjusted max HR of 180, this means he may train safely and effectively, with a great deal less heavy breathing than he thought, at a heart rate of 99–108. Of course, if a moderately higher exercise heart-rate range is well tolerated, weight loss and fitness gain will be more rapid. But the point remains that if you're truly unfit, you can start out with, and benefit from, much easier exercise than you ever dreamed possible.

Simulators to break the boredom. One of the prime reasons so many folks who start out great guns on a fitness program become exercise dropouts is boredom. And to this day, there are commercial fitness centers that open up with nothing more than a selection of strength machines and only one aerobic alternative: stationary bikes. A facility that cares about you, and wants your return business, will provide you with a wide array of aerobic (as well as strength) alternatives. And what's hot is simulators—machines that let you perform real-world aerobic activities

SPORTSPERFORMANCE

indoors, often with electronic feedback, and under professional guidance.

Stationary bikes, of course, can be considered simulators for outdoor cycling. Similarly, treadmills and rowing machines, the two other most popular indoor choices, simulate open-road running and lake/river rowing. Over the past several years, however, new simulators have found their way into fitness centers and homes.

First to market was a device known as the NordicTrack. Simulating cross-country (Nordic) skiing, and to many just as difficult to master, the device brought all the benefits of the sport indoors: upper and lower body training, true aerobic benefits, no dangerous impact trauma as in running, and no potentially excessive joint movements as in cycling (knees) or rowing (knees and low back). Following on the heels (or skis) of the NordicTrack was competitor Fitness Master. Its two models (LT-35 for the home, XC-1 for commercial settings), being far easier to master than the NordicTrack, and lower-priced, are finding their way into more and more locations. Introduced in Chicago in October 1986 was a NordicTrack-like entry from industry-leader Precor, Inc. Based on the quality of their rowers, bikes, and treadmills, their skier will be worth a try.

Not willing to leave it at Nordic-skiing simulation, Fitness Master, Inc., has just introduced an alpine-skiing simulator called the Snobound'r. A beefed-up, rectangular minitrampoline that's slightly folded in the middle, the SnoBound'r lets you jump from side to side while holding onto ski poles and keeping your torso motionless. This will offer both a low-stress aerobic workout and ski-tuning before the slopes.

After watching countless coaches (me included) run their athletes up and down stadium steps, the folks at Tri-Tech in Oklahoma brought to market the Stairmaster. Looking like a miniescalator, the model 6000 lets you climb steps in place, indoors, with a variety of computer programs or data feedback to keep you occupied. The new model 4000 PT offers even greater training variety at a lower price, though

FITNESS AND NUTRITION

at $2,000 it's mainly for commercial applications.

Ever climb a ladder and think what good exercise it is? Probably not. Anyway, it is. A company called Heart-Rate, Inc. has created a high-tech ladder climbing simulator by the same name that lets few muscles rest while training the cardiorespiratory system as well. It's not for the meek, or the novice, but it's a great way to break the boredom of that old stationary bike. Like the Stairmasters, though, Versaclimber models ranging from $2,000 to $3,200 are mostly found in commercial settings.

The value of cross-training for nontriathletes. Those strange souls who, for unknown reasons, swim a few miles in frigid seas, ride 100-plus miles cross-country, then run a full 26.2-mile marathon, made popular something called "cross-training." What's its value to you, a more rational individual? Cross-training is the careful integration of training strategies for different events—in the case of triathlons, swimming, cycling, and running. Its value to you comes from the realization that when training involves two or more activities, injuries from the relentless pounding of just one activity are reduced. That is, while you can get quite fit doing nothing but running 60 miles a week, you are likely to (a) get even more fit by devoting some of those hours to other fitness pursuits, and (b) reduce the probability of injury from all that running. In the case of Ironman triathletes, who add hundreds of miles of cycling and tens of miles of swimming to the 60 miles of running, injuries, of course, may actually increase. But for the nontriathletes, balancing your training among several aerobic options is the way to go. You'll get the details on actual combinations later.

When should you work out? Like the perennial question of where you let a 2,000-pound grizzly sit (anywhere it wants), the answer is "Anytime you want" and "Anytime you can." If you do have the luxury of choosing your workout time, however, aerobic exercise should be scheduled to maximize training and/or weight control benefits.

On the one hand, you might want to time your aerobic

(and strength) training to coincide with the high point of your daily body-temperature cycle. If you were to plot your cycle by taking a temperature every hour for 24 hours, you would notice how the peaks correspond to those times you already knew were your high-energy points, and the valleys to those low-energy points you dread and try to climb out of with coffee or sugar (yuk!). Working out during a peak time is a positively enjoyable experience, and just think: it's tough enough to work out, so why compound the problem by doing it during a low-temperature period? For those into Scrabble or big words, the study of diurnal (daily) variations in physiology is called "chronobiology."

On the other hand, if you're working out to reduce body fat, you might want to time your aerobic exercise so that it occurs during a period when your metabolism is already elevated, such as after a meal ("postprandial" for you word players). Since digestion stimulates your metabolic, or calorie-burning, rate, training a reasonable time after a meal can piggyback the calorie-burning effects of aerobic exercise.

What's a reasonable amount of time, you ask? In no case should vigorous exercise occur less than 30–45 minutes after a meal, and 60 minutes is probably the safe minimum. Of course, the larger the meal or the more vigorous the intended exercise, the longer you should wait. Since we're all different in terms of digestion time and tolerance to heavy exercise, be cautious and use a trial-and-error approach.

On the third hand (I've never felt that two hands were enough to develop a controversy fully), several exercise scientists have recommended that those trying to reduce body fat train aerobically *before* a main meal to take advantage of the appetite-dulling effects of exercise.

So what's a mother to do? Either train early or late in the day, and before or after a meal. About the only thing we know for sure is that you shouldn't eat a full meal while out jogging! Seriously, though, if you have the luxury of being able to change your workout time, do it and see what works

FITNESS AND NUTRITION

best. There will be at least one group of fitness experts who can then say "I told you so!"

THE NEWS ON NUTRITION

Much as with exercise, nutrition scientists have learned recently that *when* you eat and *how* you eat can be nearly as important as *what* you eat. There's also news in body-composition measurement, finding out just how fat or lean you really are.

WHEN TO EAT

This one is simple: the earlier the better. While we once thought that weight control was a simple matter of "calories in = calories out," it's become clear that time of day, as well as size of meal, has a great deal to do with the fate of your consumed calories. The foods you eat may either be broken down and used relatively quickly as fuel, or, in a more dastardly fashion, be chemically converted and stored for future use as fat. In the last two years, researchers have proved that eating most of your daily calories earlier in the day helps meet the demand for quick energy, so that the foods you eat early end up being used instead of being stored.

This is the death knell then for those big dinners many of us eat. The right way to eat is to chow down breakfast (remember Mom yelling at you to eat your breakfast? So much for nutrition research being the first to make this discovery!), eat a balanced and substantial lunch, and hold back at dinner. Don't try to make this change all at once, however. The smart way to do it, since it's an eating pattern foreign to your metabolic pattern, is to gradually shift amounts from later to earlier.

HOW TO EAT

Closely tied with the shift in amounts of food from later to earlier in the day is the advice to decrease the size of each meal and increase the frequency of meals and/or snacks. What? Between-meal snacks are okay? I knew I liked this book! Between-meal snacks have *always* been okay if they included the right things. Research now tells us that if we take our daily allotment of calories, say 2,400, and consume it in four 600-calorie settings, we are less likely to store any unused calories as fat than if we ate the entire 2,400 in one sitting. Call it the bathtub analogy: your tub (digestive system) can only drain (digest) a given number of gallons (calories) per hour. Fill it (feed it) at or below its drain rate and it will never overflow (store excess calories as fat). Exceed the drain rate and the tub *will* overflow (store fat).

While no one is advocating that you eat six 400-calorie, or eight 300-calorie meals a day, the concept is to eat less at your main meals and have healthy and larger-than-usual snacks. Fresh fruits, vegetables, and low-calorie yogurts are quite popular and fit the nutritional bill.

WHAT TO EAT

You'd had to have been adrift on a life raft among the islands in Micronesia to have missed the latest news on what's good to eat. I'll restrict myself here to what's hot: cold fish and monounsaturates.

Something's fishy. Well, Mom did it again. Remember (if you're old enough) cod liver oil, reportedly the world's worst-smelling substance? Mom was right again. It turns out that this cold, fatty, northern ocean fish contains an important oil compound called eicosapentanoic acid, or EPA. Because it may have beneficial effects on reducing the risk of coronary disease, EPA is a hot item at your local health-food store. But as with all things good for you, moderation is best. Consult a qualified nutritionist, dietician, or cardiologist on recommended amounts and preparations.

"If I hear the word saturated one more time...." I know you're tired of hearing about saturated and polyunsaturated fats, but there have been some recent findings on olive oil and the "monounsaturated" fats. It seems that too many polyunsaturates (liquid at room temperature, for one thing) may be as risky as too many saturates (solid at room temperature). More and more dieticians and nutritionists

are recommending greater use of monounsaturated fats, such as those found in olive oil. Again, consult an expert for the latest details.

BODY COMPOSITION

If you were on that drifting raft in Micronesia, you'd also be unaware of the importance of knowing the fat-to-lean ratio of your body when designing and fine-tuning a training regimen. There is simply no other way to know if the changes, or even lack of changes, in your weight reflect fat loss or gain, muscle loss or gain, or some combination. What is hot news is not the need for body-composition measurement, but the avalanche of new devices purporting to do the job.

Ultrasound versus impedance. Enter a local fitness center and the chances are good that you'll be offered, for about $20, the chance to have your body composition measured by either electrical impedance or ultrasound. Both are quick and painless, and theoretically more immune to error on the part of the person conducting the test (a big problem with skinfold pinches, the most common means of assessing body fat). Both require electronic devices that cost between $3,000 and $6,000, or between $2,800 to $5,800 more than a set of skinfold calipers. To pay the piper (or, more accurately, the lease payments), fitness entrepreneurs charge anywhere from $10 to $25 to zap or beep you.

Do these new devices work any better than skinfolds? Do they work at all? The book is far from closed on either technique, but at the time of this writing, the numbers looked pretty bleak for impedance and more promising for ultrasound.

Electrical impedance devices send tiny, painless electrical signals through the watery tissue of your body. Electrodes are placed on your wrists and ankles, and the conduction between the two is theoretically predictive of how much of your body weight is fat. Problem is, recent unbiased research has shown poor validity (does a test measure what it's supposed to measure?) and reliability (are the numbers constant from test to retest?). It is not uncommon for two readings taken just minutes apart to be 4% or more apart in body-fat prediction. For now, my advice is to save your $20 if offered this test.

Ultrasound devices send very high frequency sound waves into the surface layers of your body to measure body fat. A California-based company called Muscle Dynamics has a promising product called Soma-tech that has held up well to initial experimental scrutiny.

And what about hydrostatic weighing, where you are immersed in a tank of water and then cruelly asked to blow out all your air *before* waiting an additional 10 seconds? In the hands of experts, hydrostatic weighing is the gold standard against which all other techniques are evaluated. In the hands of incompetents it's just as bad as a circus guess-your-weight sideshow. In my experience, given the large number of things that can go wrong in a hydrostatic weighing procedure, and the small number of truly competent people I've seen do the technique, I'd again advise you to save your money.

That leaves us with low-tech skinfold measurements, and lower-tech circumference measurements. Skinfolds probably work as well as ultrasound when in the hands of trained pros. Circumference measurements are, in my opinion, good only for showing changes in circumference. I am *not* in favor of using them to predict body composition, because the equations used with circumferences discriminate heavily against people with big muscles.

3
THE SCIENCE OF STRENGTH

My goals in this chapter are to set the record straight on definitions and make sure that you and I are talking the same language, to present the latest in strength- and power-training theory, and to discuss the roles of free weights and various types of machines in the attainment of strength and power.

DEFINITIONS

Though this section sounds as if it belongs in a textbook, it has to be here. Strength and power training, even if you just use Nautilus equipment, are so complex you'd be lost without a definitional guidebook. Here goes:

STRENGTH

Experts like to reserve this word for one precise meaning: the ability to exert a maximum force in a single effort or repetition. Nice, clean, unambiguous.

But, alas, it's not that simple. While that definition tells you how to *measure* strength, it doesn't tell you what strength really *is*. In physical terms (you asked for it), strength is a result of the pulling power of small hooklike proteins deep within muscle. Correctly performed strength training causes muscle to grow many of these structures, called "cross-bridges," that effectively pull with greater and greater force. That's what strength is.

MUSCULAR ENDURANCE

Muscular endurance is defined as the ability to exert a submaximum force for a prolonged period of time. Again, this is an operational definition, or one that tells us how to measure the term, as opposed to a definition that tells us what muscular endurance *is*. Biologically speaking, muscular endurance results from the vigor of enzymes within muscle, and the body's ability to provide fuel for those tiny, pulling cross-bridges, so that prolonged muscular contractions can occur. In training for muscular endurance, one must keep in mind a concept known as "specificity of training." If your goal is to develop enough muscular endurance to enable you to sustain muscular effort for long periods of time, 60-second training efforts will not do it. To prepare for his world record of 52,003 consecutive sit-ups, Steve Sokol trained for hundreds of hours. One set of 12–15 repetitions, three days a week, was not "specific" to his desired training results. (Since you're probably asking if it was worth it, Steve was featured as *Cosmopolitan* magazine's Bachelor of the Month in December 1986. It *was* worth it.)

The wiser among you are still not satisfied, because I haven't addressed the paradox of how muscular endurance and strength interrelate. For example, can a person do only six push-ups, or a measly thousand sit-ups (if I didn't like Steve Sokol so much, I'd hate him!), because he/she is lacking in strength, in muscular endurance, or in both? There is no answer: it's anybody's guess. While certain interesting relationships between increasing strength and a corresponding increase in muscular endurance have been noted in some individuals, this is not always the case. Certainly, without some basic point of strength, push-ups

THE SCIENCE OF STRENGTH

or sit-ups cannot be done. At the point of 52,003 sit-ups, however, failure is more likely to be attributed to enzymes and available energy sources than a decrease in the maximum pulling power of a cross-bridge. On the other hand, how many scientists get to study cross-bridges after 52,000 sit-ups?

WORK

In physics and in the gym, "work" is nothing more than force exerted over a distance, as in 50 pounds lifted a height of one foot. The work expressed in this muscular effort would be described as "50 foot-pounds."

POWER

By introducing the time factor into the concept of work, one can express power. For example, a person lifting a 50-pound weight one foot in five seconds would obviously exert far less power than a person lifting it in one second. Since power is computed in this example as foot-pounds per second, the first person would have demonstrated a power of 10 foot-pounds per second, while the other individual would have expressed a power of 50 foot-pounds per second, a figure five times greater.

In training for power, one must again be aware of the "specificity of training" issue. While slow, high-intensity strength training, which I'll advocate in a future chapter, *does* enhance your ability to contract with force when performing at higher-than-training speeds, recent research suggests that the occasional use of faster speeds in training may be useful. More on this issue later.

CONCENTRIC OR POSITIVE CONTRACTION

When those tiny protein cross-bridges exert their pull, muscle contracts and in turn pulls on bone. Depending on which side of the limb that muscle is attached to, it may cause either a pulling or a pushing motion, but in no case can a muscle by *itself* do anything but contract. (The only muscular organ that can push by itself is the tongue, but notice that I called it a muscular "organ"—three separate muscles within the tongue, contracting simultaneously in three axes, cause pushing.) A concentric, or positive, contraction is one where the muscle shortens and causes movement of the limbs or torso.

ECCENTRIC OR NEGATIVE CONTRACTION

When some external action pulls against the shortening of the cross-bridges, and exerts a force *greater* than that which the cross-bridges exert, the muscle will lengthen. If the cross-bridges maintain their pulling efforts, but have their grip forcibly broken, the effort is known as an eccentric, negative, or "lengthening" contraction.

In practice, lowering a weight from a contracted position is a negative, or eccentric, move. When the biceps of the upper arm contracts/shortens to curl the hand toward the shoulder, it is likewise the biceps that slowly releases its tension as the external force (gravity) pulls successfully downward against the still-trying-to-contract cross-bridges. Only machines by a company known as HydraFitness offer what is called concentric-concentric exercise—the biceps contract to curl the hand upward against a hydraulic cylinder, and the triceps must then contract to push the hand downward against that cylinder. The merits of standard positive-negative exercise versus positive-positive training are still being debated.

ISOMETRIC CONTRACTION

When muscles are pitted against each other or an immovable external object, with no resulting movement, the contraction is called isometric. First introduced some 30 years ago in a hospital, where bedridden patients had no access to apparatus, isometrics do increase muscular strength. Their major shortcomings are that strength gains appear to be limited to perhaps two months of training, and that there is no easy way to quantify or put an exact number on how much force is being exerted. This makes progression, or a steady increase in the force level over consecutive workouts to keep muscle challenged and growing, quite difficult. A device known as the "Bodylink" is

THE SCIENCE OF STRENGTH

now commercially available for about $150. It offers feedback on tension levels during isometric exercise, as well as game play designed to structure such exercise. The Bodylink interfaces with a Commodore 64 computer and monitor that you provide. Contact Bodylog, Inc., at 914-241-7121 for details.

ISOTONIC CONTRACTION

This is a term that is infrequently used these days because no one is quite sure what it means. It has historically meant a muscular effort in which (a) the load being lifted is constant and (b) the muscle is free to vary in the speed of contraction. It turns out, though, that even a 50-pound barbell offers drastically varying resistance to a muscle as it moves because of the laws of physics. This phenomenon inspired several fitness inventors to create variable-resistance machines (see Chapter 5).

ISOKINETIC CONTRACTION

Here's a term with as many definitions as people trying to define it. To be truly isokinetic, a muscular contraction must (a) occur at a constant velocity and (b) work against a mechanical or electronic form of resistance that "accommodates" to the changing force output of muscle. That is, since a muscle's maximum force output changes as it contracts through a movement, a machine senses these changes and challenges the muscle accordingly.

Does isokinetic training work any better than other forms of resistive (strength) exercise? Research suggests that this is the case, but it is inconclusive. One problem is that Nautilus and similar cam-type machines are "semi-accommodative" (rather than automatically adapting to changing muscle output, they have a built-in adaptation mechanism in the shape of the cam). In any case, treat with healthy skepticism all banner headlines in fitness magazines affirming the wonders of isokinetics. Many devices that claim to be isokinetic are not. (The claim was made in one running magazine that a rubber-tubing-and-handle device was isokinetic. Please!)

SPORTSPERFORMANCE

VARIABLE-RESISTANCE TRAINING

Any device that offers resistance to a contracting muscle, in which the resistance changes as movement occurs, is a variable-resistance device. The trick is to vary resistance *accurately*, and not all devices do that. To date, not one company that manufactures cam-type variable resistance devices has made public their research, or even proved that they've done research. And that includes Nautilus Sports/Medical Industries, Inc. While we know the so-called "strength curves" of various muscles (the exact pattern in which they change in force-generating ability as they contract), we *don't* know which machines do the best job of matching those changes, and therefore are theoretically the best to train on. In this book we're going to learn Nautilus.

ATTAINING STRENGTH

So you're interested in the absolute *best* way to gain strength. Why not plan and perform a simple research study that will compare several methods and see which works best? Why not? Oh, only about 100 reasons why not. Strength research is extremely difficult because comparisons between or among groups, or even within individuals over time, are confounded by the complexity of the human organism. Since identical twins are tough to come by in numbers large enough for good strength research, you're going to have to rely largely on trial-and-error experiences, and some not-so-bad research, by us professionals.

There is general agreement that if pure strength is your goal, your strength-training efforts should be limited in the number of repetitions, but done at high intensity (heavy weights). When training with free weights, two-to-four sets of fewer-than-ten repetitions, at weights ranging from 75% to 95% of your maximum single-lift ability, are usually recommended. When using high-tech machines such as Nautilus or Cybex Eagle, which theoretically improve on the efficiency of free weights, a great deal of experience has shown that one perfectly performed set of 12-15 repetitions,

THE SCIENCE OF STRENGTH

plus several additional negative reps, is enough for maximum strength gains.

This has never been easy to swallow for advocates of free-weight training, who have in general been pretty bullheaded about the concept of one set of 12-15 reps being a sufficient training stimulus. No matter. Those of us who worked at and traveled for Nautilus, and who have observed hundreds or perhaps thousands of individuals train in that single-set fashion, know it works. I've personally trained that way, and taught hundreds of trainers to train members that way. And to date, in late 1986, four years after I left Nautilus and moved north, I have yet to hear any negative feedback. For more than four years I have heard nothing but "Boy, am I pleased with the results of your training advice," and I've heard that comment often. Having applied this training philosophy to the old and the young, world-class athletes and nonathletes, I'm convinced enough to recommend it without hesitation. Perhaps someday there will be some research to back me up, but I'm not waiting.

DEVELOPING POWER

Stating that 12-15 reps performed at slow speed on a Nautilus machine will increase muscular power is an even tougher pill to swallow for many strength-training professionals. Having seen it work, however, I remain a strong advocate. It must be noted, however, that in all cases where I observed significant performance increases attributable in part to Nautilus training, there has been quality coaching as well, with athletes devoting pool or track time to power-oriented performance drills. I have *not* observed swimmers or runners train on Nautilus while abstaining from running or swimming, then go out after nine weeks and break personal records.

What does this all mean? My guess is that power, which you recall from a few pages ago involves work done over time, really requires some "speed-specific" training. That is, unless the motor-control system in your brain, and the muscles themselves, are given some opportunity to create large amounts of force in short periods of time, you may not see the power gains you'd like. This requires either combining slow training on Nautilus equipment with higher-speed power training on the field, or perhaps use of machines in the gym or weight room that allow safe, effective, high-speed training. Currently, the only machines that fit the bill in this author's mind are manufactured by the Keiser Company in Fresno, California. You'll know their machines as either CAM II (first generation), Keiser K200 (second generation), or K300 (third generation).

Rather than using iron plates, which do not allow high-speed training because of the momentum/inertia problem, Keiser uses compressed air. Through ingenious valving and linkages, you can train safely and effectively at quite high speeds without ever "throwing" the weight, as you would with a barbell or a Nautilus or Eagle machine. Good fitness centers will offer both air and weight-stack machines to expand your training options.

How might you use Keiser air machines to develop power? Though that's not really a subject for this book, I suggest you work with progressively heavier weights, at progressively higher speeds, and with steadily increasing reps over time.

4
COMBINING STRENGTH AND AEROBIC CONDITIONING

Yes, I know this is a Nautilus book. And I know some of you are wondering why I keep bringing up aerobic exercise. Well, I have two primary reasons. First, if you're after well-defined muscles and an impressive overall shape, all the Nautilus training on Earth won't reduce body fat enough for your muscles or silhouette to wow members of the opposite sex. Strength work *must* be combined with fat-burning aerobic exercise to sculpt you effectively.

Second, and more important (in my mind, at least, but then I don't get to look at your biceps or buns every day), is the greater contribution to general health and well-being made by aerobic exercise. Strength is certainly important, but it's aerobic work that enhances heart and lung function and evidently serves to reduce the risk of an ever-growing list of illnesses and degenerative conditions. Great buns or biceps aren't of much use if you're in a coffin at age 40 because of a fatal coronary.

My goal in this chapter is to explain what aerobic exercise *really* is, offer a set of guidelines that will enable you to write and safely carry out your own aerobic-exercise prescription, then show you the way to safely combine strength and aerobic training.

WHAT MAKES AN EXERCISE AEROBIC?

The answer is not "When someone says it's aerobic," although judging from books and videotapes coming out of Hollywood, you would think that just saying so is the only criterion necessary. An exercise is only aerobic if *all four* of these criteria are met:

1. You are using the large muscle groups of the leg (front thigh, or quadriceps; back thigh, or hamstrings; buttocks, or gluteals) or midback (latissimus dorsi).
2. These muscles are being used rhythmically and repetitively, as in cycling.
3. Such rhythmic motions occur for eight or more consecutive minutes.
4. Your heart rate is elevated into an age- and fitness-related range known as the target zone.

If all four criteria aren't met, what you're doing ain't aerobic. Period. What's more, these rules simply ensure that the exercise can be called aerobic. In fact, you don't gain aerobic *benefits* until you've been going rhythmically and repetitively for at least 12 minutes.

Here's the list of activities that clearly meet all four criteria without footnotes:

- Walking/jogging/running
- Stationary cycling
- Rope jumping
- Stair- or ladder-climbing
- Ice- and roller-skating
- Nordic skiing
- Rowing

The activities in this table may fulfill all four criteria under the right conditions:

STRENGTH AND AEROBICS

Activity	Caveats
Swimming	As offered in most fitness centers, where 40-foot pools are the norm, swimming is not aerobic. Your pool should be at least 60 feet long.
Outdoor Cycling	If you're in the country and can pedal without extensive coasting, okay. Inner-city cycling is not aerobic.
Aerobic Dance	Choreography must include repetitive use of the lower body, a rule frequently violated.
Racquet Sports	Evenly matched partners who rally for extended periods of time may receive aerobic benefits.
Rebounders	Only fitness novices appear to get measurable aerobic benefit.
Circuit Weight Training	Aerobic devices must be inserted between strength machines to ensure aerobic benefits.

THE BENEFITS OF TRUE AEROBIC EXERCISE, or ALL THINGS COME TO THOSE WHO TRAIN

At least twice now I have touted the benefits of aerobic exercise for general health and weight control. There's more to it than just 12 minutes a day, though. While research has established that particular number as the *minimum* for gaining benefits, a serious body-fat reduction program requires a greater time commitment. Scientists now believe that the hormones that find and break down stored body fat for use in aerobic exercise aren't freely flowing until you've been going at it rhythmically and repetitively for at least 25 minutes. While 12 minutes a day is something to be proud of, and while it will have positive effects on body fat, it's just not enough.

One of the initially hidden but wonderful benefits of both aerobic and strength exercise is their enhancing effect on basal metabolic rate (BMR). This is a deal you can't refuse: even while you're reading or relaxing, your body will be churning along at a higher calorie-burning rate than before you started training. Should you maintain your caloric intake where it was before training, this BMR boost, plus the calories you burn while exercising, should make fat loss a relative snap. When you're satisfied with your level of body fat, your quickened BMR and exercise-induced calorie-burning rate will allow you to safely eat more (music to most of our ears).

If you're not convinced by now, skip the next section, go directly past GO (forget the $200), and start the Nautilus chapters. If I've made my case and you're still interested, what follows is a step-by-step guide to writing an exercise prescription.

WRITING AN AEROBIC EXERCISE PRESCRIPTION

A comprehensive exercise plan is known as an exercise prescription. Its four components are:

- Type of exercise
- Intensity of exercise
- Duration of exercise
- Frequency of exercise

Let's analyze them one by one.

TYPE OF EXERCISE

From the list of true aerobic exercises presented above, your choice will be based on availability, likes and dislikes, your fitness level, and potential orthopedic problems. While the first two considerations are self-explanatory, the second two aren't.

If you're at a low level of fitness, you'd be well advised to

STRENGTH AND AEROBICS

stick with lower-intensity choices such as walking (treadmill or outdoors), stationary cycling, or cross-country skiing (legs only). As you progress, you can more safely try rowing, climbing simulators, and rope jumping.

If you have a problem with your ankles, shins, knees, hips, low back, or shoulders, your aerobic choices will be limited. While rowing machines are the fastest-growing category in home exercise equipment sales, they can be quite tough on knees and backs. Aerobic dance programs claiming to be low- or nonimpact frequently aren't, nor are they aerobic. Don't invest in home equipment, or join a commercial center that doesn't have lots of aerobic choices, until you consider all these factors.

Is there one *best* choice? Most experts rate cross-country skiing as number one because it requires full-body involvement and yields the greatest improvements in cardiovascular capacity, yet requires no excessive flexions or extensions of the limbs or back, and no pounding the way jogging/running does. Live too far south for the real thing? Give the Fitness Master, NordicTrack, or Precor simulators a try.

INTENSITY OF EXERCISE

What to measure. Intensity can be measured in several ways, such as how fast you're moving or how much resistance you're working against. The problem is, these data are arbitrary and don't tell you anything about how your body, during each workout, is *responding* to that mechanical or electronic challenge. If you've ever worked out, you know that an intensity level that feels good one day may feel miserably hard or ridiculously easy the next. My advice is to always monitor your heart-rate response *as well as* the mechanical intensity. Each phase of each aerobic workout is then fine-tuned, intensity being adjusted up or down according to your physiological readiness at that instant.

Measuring heart-rate response. Although electronic pulse monitors, ranging in price (and effectiveness) from $39 to $329, make things easy, you can accurately take your pulse with your index and middle fingers. Press gently

SPORTSPERFORMANCE

along either the side of your trachea (windpipe) or the tendons along the thumb side of your wrist until you find your pulse. Research has shown that, with care, six-, ten-, or fifteen-second pulse counts are equally accurate in estimating beats per minute. The advantage of a six-second pulse count is that the full-minute pulse is obtained by simply adding a zero to the number. Rusty on your math? Since a minute pulse would be obtained by multiplying the six-second count by ten, all you need to do is add the zero.

Instructors in many fitness centers use a ten-second pulse count, fearing the potential error in the six-second version. If you take care, and count carefully, six seconds should work fine.

How high the intensity? The answer depends almost totally on your age- and fitness-adjusted "target heart-rate zone." As you age, the maximum rate your heart can beat declines about one beat a year. The universally used estimate of age-adjusted max is 220 minus age). Using this figure, scientists have set these guidelines for finding your target zone, that pulse range in which you are getting danger-free aerobic benefits.

If you consider yourself	as defined by	multiply your Max HR by
Totally unfit	No exercise history	.55 to .65
Beginner level	Less than 3 months	.60 to .70
Intermediate fitness	4-6 months steady	.65 to .75
Moderately-to-highly fit	6-9 months steady	.70 to .80
Very fit, athlete	12 months or more	.75 to .85+

For example, a 40-year-old who considers himself intermediate in fitness (has been in strength and aerobic train-

STRENGTH AND AEROBICS

ing for six months) would find his aerobic target zone in this manner:

1. Max HR = 220 − 40 = 180
2. 0.65 × 180 = 117 ; 0.75 × 180 = 135
3. Target HR Zone = 117 to 135

By training aerobically with your heart rate in this range, you reduce the risk of overtraining or a coronary accident, while ensuring weight control and full benefits to the cardiovascular system. Most people are shocked by how low this zone turns out to be, for we have a national misconception that if you're not huffing, puffing, and ready to throw up, exercise can't be doing any good. Wrong, wrong, wrong.

Perceived exertion. As I noted earlier, you're bound to have good days and bad days, when even the low side of your target zone feels like too much. The rule: always listen to your body. When your level of "perceived exertion," or how strenuous it actually feels, is uncomfortably high, slow down. *Never* stop dead in your tracks (excuse the expression), because the body diverts most of its blood supply to exercising muscles, and coming to a complete stop can leave you with most of the blood pooled in your legs (especially if you've been running or cycling). This puts a tremendous strain on the heart, and can have fatal consequences. *Always slow down gradually, allowing the muscles to perform a built-in function known as "milking," whereby as they contract they squeeze blood back toward the heart through one-way valves in the veins. Intense aerobic exercise should be followed without exception by at least a five-minute easy cool-down (more on that later).*

DURATION OF EXERCISE

Allow me to repeat myself: if it's body-fat reduction you're after, you're going to have to crank away for 25 or more minutes in your target zone to ensure a flow of fat-

SPORTSPERFORMANCE

mobilizing hormones. If you're satisfied with your current body-fat levels, and are either interested in the general health benefits of aerobic exercise or are an athlete in training for an aerobic event, you'll get satisfactory benefits from 15 to 30 minutes of target-zone training, and more benefits from 30 to 45 minutes. Once everyone but competitive athletes gets past 45 minutes of target-zone aerobics, most scientists believe there are diminishing returns.

The boredom-beating news here is that there's no reason to spend all that target-zone time doing just one aerobic activity. As long as the four cardinal rules of aerobic exercise are adhered to, you can string together, for example, 12 minutes of cycling, 12 of rowing, 12 of running, and 12 of stair climbing into a superb and anything-but-boring 48-minute workout.

Warm-ups and cool-downs. I hope you noticed the 40 or so times I used the phrase "minutes of target-zone training." These recommended time intervals are exclusive of the critical five-minute warm-up and five-minute cool-down. Warm-ups, while we're on the subject, are best performed on the same apparatus you're going to train on. Start off at a gentle pace and intensity, and increase both gradually until your heart rate just reaches the bottom of your target zone at the five-minute mark. When cooling down you can abruptly decrease intensity and pace.

Lasting the duration. So how do I expect you, who hasn't trained in (give or take) 10 years, or maybe ever, to last 25 minutes in your target zone? There are essentially two ways, though the more unfit among you have only one choice.

Assuming you can tolerate 12 minutes of target HR zone aerobic training, your first choice is simply to add one or two minutes to your workout each week, or every fourth workout. This gradual progression is a successful means to reach the 25–30 minute mark. But what choice do you have if you can't even make the 12-minute minimum? Through the semimagic of "interval training," the rhythmic alterna-

STRENGTH AND AEROBICS

tion of exercise and rest intervals, you'll be at the 12-minute, and even 25-minute, mark before you know it. And because interval training can also be used by the fit, those of you who are able to do the 12-minute minimum can use "intervals" to boost exercise duration. But before I get into a long digression on interval training, here's the fourth variable in your exercise prescription.

FREQUENCY OF EXERCISE

Scientists have almost conclusively determined that the minimum training frequency for measurable aerobic benefits is three workouts a week. Once you've reached a desired level of aerobic fitness, that level can be maintained with two properly structured workouts a week. If you're an athlete in training, or someone trying to make a serious inroad into stored body fat, you may be able to tolerate, and will derive additional benefits from, four to six workouts a week. Such a high training frequency carries with it, however, the risks of overtraining-induced injury or illness. Be on the lookout for these signs of overtraining:

- A rise in morning resting heart rate
- Growing lethargy
- Sudden changes in appetite or body weight
- Decrease in sleep quality; increase in difficulty falling asleep or waking
- Nagging injuries that heal less quickly than expected

The appearance of two or more of these warning signs is cause for immediate reduction in training frequency, intensity, and duration.

WRITING YOUR AEROBIC EXERCISE PRESCRIPTION

To review, your prescription must specify four factors:

type, intensity, duration, and frequency of exercise. Follow this path to write your prescription:

1. Consult a doctor about starting a program if you haven't spoken to one recently.
2. Plan your weekly schedule to include the desired frequency of workouts in time slots you won't easily be able to cancel. If you schedule workouts at times you know will be difficult to work with, you're in trouble.
3. Analyze what you want and need to accomplish through aerobic exercise so you may accurately set the remaining variables.
4. Carefully select a fitness center to join, or carefully consider the purchase of home aerobic equipment, based on your previous exercise equipment likes and dislikes, the health of your joints and low back, and your level of fitness. Choose one or two types of aerobic exercise that seems a "best fit."
5. Plot your target heart-rate zone. Study how to set intensity on the machines you'll be using.
6. Try for the minimum 12 minutes in the target zone, plus a five-minute warm-up and cool-down. If you cannot make it, read the "Interval Training" section and try again. If you can make it, either add one to two minutes a week until you reach your duration goal, or use interval-training strategies to increase the duration.

INTERVAL TRAINING
WHY USE INTERVALS?

There are three great reasons to read this section carefully:

1. Beginners, as discussed earlier, can instantly tolerate a 12-minute or longer workout by properly structuring exercise bouts and rest intervals.

STRENGTH AND AEROBICS

2. The number of interval-training prescriptions, or "ITPs," you can dream up is infinite. This is probably the best way to beat the boredom problem. The way you're most likely training now is called "continuous," a boring ride/run/row that's nonstop from warm-up to cool-down. Intervals can provide new challenges each workout.
3. Periodic rest intervals have the powerful effect of letting you train at higher intensity, and longer at that intensity, than would be otherwise possible. It is safe to say that no elite athlete on earth trains without intervals, for intervals clearly enhance performance.

WHAT IS INTERVAL TRAINING?

Now that I've sold you on it, I ought to tell you what you've bought. Interval training is the alternation between exercise bouts and rest periods. Cycling for 60 seconds, resting for 30 seconds, then repeating that cycle nine more times would be written in interval-training lingo as:

$$10 \times :60 \text{ (:30 rest)}$$

Adding information on exercise intensity and the type of rest gives you the full interval-training prescription (ITP).

Beginners usually use interval training to increase exercise duration. Their initial ITP specifies short work bouts and long rest intervals, which let the body recover from the rigors of exercise. Over time, the work intervals are lengthened and the rest intervals shortened. Novices might progress from an ITP of *10 × :10 (:50 rest)* during their first week on a stationary bike to *10 × :50 (:10 rest)* during the fifth week.

Athletes, or those who are already fit, also benefit from the periodic opportunities to partially recover from intense work intervals. Using treadmill running as an example, you might now be capable of running four miles at an eight-minute-mile pace. With an ITP of *16 × .25 mile (:30 rest) at 7:30 pace*, you'd cover four miles at a significantly faster pace. The training secret elite athletes use is the

SPORTSPERFORMANCE

gradual reduction of the 30-second rest intervals, so that after perhaps six weeks of a five-second-per-week reduction in the rest intervals, you'd be running four continuous miles at 7:30 per mile!

WRITING YOUR ITP

Not coincidentally, an ITP has the same four variables as

EXERCISE TYPE	INTENSITY FEEDBACK	BEGINNER	INTERMEDIATE	ADVANCED
Cycling	Rpm/mph	60/12	70-80/15-20	80+/20+
	Numerical readout (1-10)	1-3	4-6	7-10
	Watts (power)	25-75	75-150	100+
	Calories/hr	up to 400	400-750	750+
Rowing	Strokes/minute	up to 20	20-30	30+
	Simple readout (1-6)	1-2	3-6	3-6
	Watts	25-75	75-150	100+
	Calories/hr	up to 400	400-750	750+
Running	Mph (W = walk; J = jog; R = run)	W up to 4	J/R 5-7	R 6+
	Percent incline	up to 5%	up to 10%	10%+
Swimming	Yards/minute	up to 50	50-75	75+
Jump Rope	Turns/minute	20-40	40-60	60+

STRENGTH AND AEROBICS

your general aerobic-exercise prescription: type, intensity, duration, and frequency.

Exercise type. Considerations here are identical to those described previously.

Exercise intensity. Most of the thought in writing an ITP goes into intensity and duration planning. Always start conservatively, because the almost sure result of doing too much too soon is injury.

The intensity you specify in your ITP depends on the type of exercise you'll be performing and the type of feedback on the actual workload or performance level that's available. As you can see in the table, intensity information can range from a simple and subjective "easy, moderate, or hard" to digitally displayed data on everything, right up to the weather in Anchorage. Before attempting to write your ITP, scout out the equipment you'll be using, or assess the activity, and write down the type of intensity information available.

Adjusting the intensity variable during a workout, or afterward for the next workout, is once again based on two things: heart-rate response and perceived exertion. If the intensity level you prescribe keeps your heart rate in its correct zone, and you perceive the level of exertion as acceptable, great. If things are too easy or too rough, adjust the intensity variable accordingly.

Use this table of intensity range guidelines for five of the most common aerobic exercises.

EXERCISE DURATION

What you'll manipulate here is the "work/rest ratio," or the amount of exercise time and rest time. A work/rest ratio of 3/1 means your exercise bout will last three times as long as your rest interval. Conversely, a ratio of 1/3 means that the rest interval is three times as long as the work interval.

For beginners. Your duration variable is quite conservatively set. To make your initial 12 minutes, work/rest ratios of 1/5 are a good place to start. Ten-second work bouts combined with 50-second rest intervals fill out one revolution of the second hand. After one week, increase the work bouts to :15 and the rest intervals to :45, keeping the number

SPORTSPERFORMANCE

of cycles constant at 12. Week 3 takes you to :20/:40, and Week 4 to :25/:35. By the time you reach :50/:10, you'll probably be capable of a straight, rest-free 12 minutes. At this point, you can stick with continuous training for a while, adding 30 seconds or more a week until you reach the duration goal of your aerobic-exercise prescription, or stick with intervals and change the prescription. One choice might be a work/rest ratio of 1:00/:45, progressing by reducing the rest interval five seconds a week but keeping the work bout constant. As you can see, as long as you watch your heart-rate response and pay attention to perceived exertion, only your imagination limits you in writing ITPs.

For intermediate and advanced persons. You folks also have unlimited potential in structuring the duration variable of your ITP. If you're interested in sprinting and the development of anaerobic power, your work/rest ratios will run from 1/3 up to 1/10 or more. High-quality (high-speed) training, followed by lots of rest, for several repeated cycles, is a proven way to get fast and powerful.

If you're training for a specific distance or event, your work/rest ratio can be specifically tailored as in the example given earlier for dropping a four-mile run from an 8:00 to a 7:30 pace.

In general, work/rest ratios for the fit range from 2/1 to 8/1. Runners on a track might do 10 reps of running a quarter (440 yards), then walk the next curve (about 80 yards); or on a treadmill do 10 reps of a .25 mile run and a .10 mile walk. Swimmers can swim 50s (two laps of a 25-yard pool) or 100s with as little as 10 to 30 seconds rest, or do what is called "swimming on the clock," starting another 50- or 100-yard swim every one or two minutes, resting after the finish of one rep until the second hand reaches 60. If a 50 takes you 45 seconds, for example, swimming "on a minute" would give you 15 seconds rest. The faster you swim, the more rest you're entitled to.

Work/rest ratios can change even during each of the three phases of an aerobic workout (warm-up, target zone, and cool-down). You might start with a few minutes of easy,

STRENGTH AND AEROBICS

continuous work, proceed from a low or even reverse work/rest ratio (1/2 up to 2/1), to higher and higher ratios, then cool down in reverse order. Here's an example for rope jumping:

Phase	Work/Rest Data	Intensity	Ratio
Warm-up	(5×) :10 jump/:20 rest	80 turns/min	1/2
Target Zone	(5×) :30 jump/:30 rest	100 turns/min	1/1
	(5×) :45 jump/:15 rest	100 turns/min	3/1
	(5×) :30 jump/:30 rest	100 turns/min	1/1
Cool-down	(5×) :10 jump/:20 rest	80 turns/min	1/2
Walk	5:00		

Total Training Time: 20:00 plus walk

The matter of rest. Wait—we're not done with the duration variable just yet. ITPs are so versatile that you can even specify the kind of rest you should take. "Inactive" rest, or what you thought I was talking about all along, is complete inactivity. It's recommended for beginners and for those athletes who are training for nonaerobic (anaerobic) power events, such as 100- and 200-meter runs, and 50- and 100-yard or -meter swims. "Active" rest, wherein you move at low speed and intensity during your rest intervals (walking or easy pedaling, for example), can be used at any time, but is particularly useful in keeping you from getting stiff or cold between work bouts.

FREQUENCY OF REPETITIONS

This is the fourth and final variable in writing your ITP. As opposed to the "three times a week" kind of frequency, we're referring here to how many work/rest cycles you're going to perform. The number you choose is intimately related to the duration variable, for if your goal is 25 minutes, and your guess as to a tolerable work/rest ratio is :30/:30, you have no choice but to do 25 reps. My advice is to let the frequency variable generally follow the decision

SPORTSPERFORMANCE

on work/rest ratio and desired total workout duration. There is no reason you can't do as few as four repetitions, or as many as 100. I'll never forget witnessing the U.S. Merchant Marine Academy swim team pacing through a hundred, 100-yard freestyle swims. (I guess it was preparation in the event they capsized 10,000 yards from shore.)

SPEEDPLAY OR "FARTLEK" TRAINING

Usually considered a type of interval training, speedplay ("fartlek" denotes its Scandinavian origin) is the alternation between easy and hard exercise bouts during a continuous interval. A 1,000-yard swim, for example, swum in one-lap-easy, one-lap-hard fashion would fall under the "speedplay" designation. If you're willing to call the easy bouts "active rest," you'll consider speedplay a type of interval training.

COMBINING AEROBIC AND STRENGTH TRAINING

No, I haven't forgotten about strength training.

The rules to follow in combining strength and aerobic training are pretty simple. The first thing that must be done (just as in life!) is priority setting. The way you plot your week of workouts depends on whether you place a higher priority on strength or aerobic benefits.

For the vain. If you should decide that big biceps or tight buns are more important than a healthy heart, (a) shame on you, and (b) follow these guidelines:

- *Never* do an aerobic workout immediately after your strength workout.
- Immediately precede a strength workout with an aerobic workout only if you have *no* alternative.
- The best schedule is aerobics in the morning and strength in the afternoon.
- The second-best schedule is strength and aerobics on alternating days (M-W-F for strength, Tu-Th-Sa for aerobics).

STRENGTH AND AEROBICS

Is there a method to this madness? You bet. To maximize your gains from strength training, you'll want to train when you're rested and fresh, and not overstress muscles by working out aerobically right after your strength training. Allow as much time as possible for muscle proteins to grow after a strength bout. Training aerobically in the morning and then for strength in the evening gives you about 36 hours of rest, assuming a three-days-a-week schedule.

For the less vain (and more aerobically inclined). Should you decide that aerobic benefits are more important than strength or muscle-size gains, follow these guidelines:

- Promise not to be too jealous of those with bigger biceps or tighter buns (though aerobics can do great things for buns).
- *Never* do a strength workout immediately before an aerobic workout.
- If it's body-fat reduction you're after, strength work may safely follow an aerobic workout that session, that day, or the next day.
- If you want to improve your aerobic capacity, the best strategy is strength in the morning and aerobics in the afternoon, followed by 36 hours of rest. Second best is alternate days. Third best, which many people are left with, is aerobics first, strength second in one club visit.

Now if that isn't everything you ever wanted to know about aerobic exercise, and how to combine it with strength training, that's too bad. This chapter's over.

5
INTRODUCTION TO NAUTILUS TRAINING

A BRIEF HISTORICAL PERSPECTIVE

It's been only quite recently that other strength equipment manufacturers have made inroads into Nautilus Sports/Medical Industries' dominance of the market. Two years ago, you couldn't find a fitness center or gym with anything *but* Nautilus machines. Even with the strong sales of Keiser and Cybex Eagle machines, though, the name "Nautilus" is still used almost universally, like the phrase, "Make a Xerox." Why?

To be honest, no one knows the answer in detail. Much of the early attraction to Nautilus stemmed from its use by professional athletes and bodybuilders. An even greater measure of its success has been attributed to the serendipity of being in the right place at the right time. Here are these intimidating, complex pieces of equipment that promise strength, size, and power, and here comes America in the mid-1970s, with its awakening exercise consciousness. Boom! "I train on Nautilus" becomes the thing to say when exercise comes up in conversation. The company's success is *not* due to advertising, marketing, or anything planned. From my discussions with people around at the beginning,

INTRODUCTION TO NAUTILUS

and from what I saw in my tenure as research coordinator, Nautilus had a good product when a good product was needed, and the rest was alchemy.

VARIABLE RESISTANCE TRAINING

Many people claim to have originated the concept of variable resistance and the devices that bring about the variation. Arthur Jones, the man who founded Nautilus Sports/Medical Industries, Inc., in 1970 in Lake Helen, Florida, is one of those claimants. Whether he did or not matters little to us here; suffice to say that the machines his company has manufactured over the last 16 years have made variable resistance indispensable for high-tech strength training.

Why is variable resistance necessary? As I noted earlier, when a muscle contracts through its range of motion, it experiences changes in its maximum "strength" at each point. Because of a combination of its internal structure and how it attaches to bone, a muscle may get progressively "stronger" as it contracts, progressively "weaker," or go from weak to strong to weak. While the quadriceps on the front thigh, for example, follows the latter pattern, the hamstring on the back of the thigh starts strong (with the leg fully extended) and shows a progressive decrease in maximum force as the heel nears the buttocks.

This variation in muscle force output during a movement raises a serious theoretical question with regard to the accepted concept of overloading a muscle to make it grow: if a muscle has one or more weak points during a movement, how can a heavy-enough weight ever be lifted to overload that muscle in its strongest position? For instance, if the biceps of the upper arm can create no more than 40 pounds of force when it begins a curling movement, but can create 80 pounds of force if measured at the midpoint of the curl, how can one lift more than a 40-pound weight? And if one *can't*, what implications does that have for efficient strength training?

SPORTSPERFORMANCE

Before answering that last question, let's discuss the difference between "theoretical" and "practical" implications. I am convinced from a theoretical standpoint that barbells and simple pulley-type weight machines cannot possibly work because they can't provide correct variable resistance. Speaking practically, I know that men and women for years have been getting big, strong, and powerful from these theoretically useless devices. While the concept of "correct variable resistance" as espoused by Nautilus, Eagle, and others makes scientific sense, it's not enough reason to give up totally on other forms of strength training.

In any case, the Nautilus machines you're about to use employ a strangely shaped, rotating device called a cam. Cams, unlike conventionally round wheels, do not have a fixed radius. Rather, the radius may change according to the whim of whoever machines the cam. According to the laws of physics, if you pull a weight stack and chain over this cam that has a constantly varying radius, the resistance, or "effective load" of the weight stack, will vary. Theoretically, by precisely measuring the strength variation in a muscle as it works, and then machining the shape of the cam to match that variation, you can create a device that offers perfect variable resistance.

What would this machine feel like? It would, with one selected amount of weight, offer less resistance when your muscle was in a weak position, and more resistance when it was in a strong position. Would this more perfectly overload the muscle and lead to faster and greater training gains? Theoretically, yes. Practically, no one knows for sure. There is zippo research one way or the other.

Experience, though, as I've told you earlier, *does* support the theoretical advantage of Nautilus and other variable resistance machines. While no one ever claims to get terrific results from just *one set* of a free-weight exercise, that claim has not only been made but substantiated countless times

INTRODUCTION TO NAUTILUS

(many by me personally) on Nautilus equipment. My gut feeling is that variable resistance *does* make a difference.

This apparent ability to reduce the number of sets and repetitions, and therefore training time, to a bare minimum, led someone at Nautilus to describe their products as "Time Machines." A phrase I've used countless times to describe Nautilus training is, similarly, "time-efficient fitness." I don't believe you can do it with free weights or pulley-type machines.

AND IN THE FURTHER INTEREST OF TIME EFFICIENCY...

Arthur Jones was unquestionably the first to design and produce machines featuring two complementary movements for the advanced training of one muscle. Calling his idea the "preexhaustion principle," Jones reasoned as follows: if a muscle is optimally stimulated to grow by one brief, intense set of repetitions that take it to momentary "failure," why not pair exercises in one machine that can wring every ounce of contractile force out of that muscle? The trick is to employ a second movement that uses *two* sets of muscles—the primary target muscle that was trained directly during the first exercise, and a second, fresh muscle that was *unused* during the first movement. Lost? (I think I was when this was first explained to me.) This chart shows Mr. Jones' devilish "compound machines" that employ the preexhaustion principle for maximum training agony, as well as gains. Note that in each case, the second movement adds a fresh muscle to the one "preexhausted" in the first movement. Having them built into one unit allows you to go rapidly from the first to the second, preventing the prime muscle from recovering even slightly. To use Jones' favorite word, it's "brutal." But if it's results you're after, this is the best way.

SPORTSPERFORMANCE

Machine	Component Exercises	Muscles Worked
Compound Leg	Leg Extension	Quadriceps
	Leg Press	Quads, Hamstrings, Gluteals
Behind Neck/ Torso Arm	Behind Neck	Latissimus
	Torso Arm	Lats, Biceps, Brachialis
Pullover/ Torso Arm	Pullover	Latissimus
	Torso Arm	Lats, Biceps, Brachialis
Double Shoulder	Lateral Raise	Deltoids
	Overhead Press	Deltoids, Triceps
Double Chest	Arm Cross	Pectoralis
	Decline Press	Pectoralis, Triceps

TRAINING STRATEGY

TRAINING INTENSITY AND SETS

The keystone of the Nautilus training philosophy is "one set to momentary muscular failure," and it bears explaining. Nautilus founder Jones often says, "It took me 20 years to learn that two sets are better than four, and another 20 to learn that one set is better than two." That ultimate, single set of repetitions that Jones came up with, though, is not a meandering, unmotivated 12-15 repetitions—it's maximally intense, focused, and taken to the point where no additional repetitions can be performed in perfect form, or "momentary muscular failure." (This is *not*, by the way, to be interpreted as momentary failure of the heart muscle, for

INTRODUCTION TO NAUTILUS

strength results don't require *that* big a sacrifice.) How much weight is considered "maximally intense"? Through trial and error, you're going to spend about four workouts finding a weight on each machine that you can no longer move in perfect form after having performed 12–15 reps.

Is it for you? If this is your first exposure to Nautilus theory, and you haven't actually gotten on a machine yet to *feel* momentary muscular failure, let me tell you that it's significantly less pleasant than two weeks in Maui with the man or woman of your dreams. In fact, many of you will choose to forgo "one set to failure" for two rationally performed sets at 80% or 90% of your maximum ability. It's likely, though unproved, that you'll derive the same benefits. It's definite that (a) you'll hurt less and (b) spend more time in the gym. Your choice! If you've been identified as hypertensive, or having any of the other coronary risk factors listed below, two less-intense sets are your prescription.

THE CORONARY RISK FACTORS
- Hypertension
- Smoking
- Obesity
- Family History of Heart Disease
- Sedentary Lifestyle
- High Stress Levels
- Diabetes

THE NUMBER OF REPETITIONS

Beginners and Intermediates. For a change we're going to have to rely on experience rather than research, though at some point, so much experience has been amassed and recorded that it is considered research. The great majority of folks who have trained on Nautilus have gotten all the results they wanted from performing one set of 12 to 15 reps before reaching momentary muscular failure. This doesn't mean that once you get to the 15th rep you jump off the machine and head for the next one. The goal (if it's appropriate for you) is training to failure, which may mean

SPORTSPERFORMANCE

10 reps one workout and 18 the next. In general, when you can perform 15 reps in perfect form for two consecutive workouts, you've mastered that weight. Increase the resistance by 5 to 10 pounds next workout. (You'll know 10 pounds is too much if you can't complete eight reps.)

The compound machines. Consider Nautilus compound machines as two complete exercises, and as such, shoot for 12-15 reps on each, setting your weights accordingly.

For advanced trainees and athletes. You're not finished when you get to rep 15. What you've got in store is advanced negative training. (The wiser among you will skip this section to avoid the muscular pain—but good pain—that is sure to follow.) By using these honeys carefully on a regular basis you'll be almost guaranteed top training gains.

TYPE OF TRAINING	CAN BE USED
Negative-Only Only the target muscle performs the eccentric phase of the movement.	By itself After 12-15 reps
Negative-Accentuated One leg or arm helps with concentric phase, other performs eccentric rep.	By itself After 12-15 reps
Negative-Emphasized Spotter adds his or her own resistance to the eccentric phase.	After 12-15 reps

Your standard set, if you're willing and able and have a training partner or spotter, will be structured as follows:

- 12-15 standard reps to momentary muscular failure;
- 2-4 negative-only repetitions; and, optionally,
- 2-4 negative-emphasized reps.

INTRODUCTION TO NAUTILUS

While this might be classified by some psychiatrists as clinically psychotic, it works.

How often can or should you try negative-only sets or even entire negative-only workouts? Negative-only sets should consist of about 10 reps, and the weight should be lowered to a count of about 10. Of the two or three workouts you'll do each week, I'd try no more than one negative-only set with each exercise. Negative-only workouts, where all machines are used without positive or concentric work, might be attempted once every two weeks.

HOW MANY MACHINES?

A full workout is considered to include anywhere from 10 to 14 machines (remember that compound machines count as two). Do not devote more than two machines to the same muscle or muscle group.

SPEED OF TRAINING

"Slow" and "controlled" are the operative words for the speed-of-training issue. Since human muscle is 30%–40% stronger when lowering a weight (eccentric or negative phase), you should ensure maximum overload by lowering the weight more slowly than you lift it. This "fools" the muscle into thinking it is lowering more weight than it is lifting. Rather than give you hard-and-fast timing suggestions, I'll simply state that the weight stack should travel upward slowly and under control, and be lowered even more slowly. (If you insist, this will mean about 2–3 seconds on the positive stroke, and 3–4 seconds on the negative.)

SPEED BETWEEN MACHINES

Depending on the crowds in your facility, advice here may be moot. No matter, be aware that strength gains are maximized if you rest several minutes between machines, and metabolic gains (not true aerobic gains, but improvements in heart and lung function and muscular endurance) will be maximized if you move rapidly from machine to machine.

Sparing you the full explanation, I will say that an

intense Nautilus circuit may quickly elevate your heart rate into its target zone, and keep it there for 20 minutes or more, but it's not aerobic. This point is obvious from our earlier four rules on what makes an exercise aerobic, and has been proven by several research studies. Inserting aerobic bouts of three to six minutes between machines, however, *has* been demonstrated to yield true aerobic benefits. This type of training regimen is called a "super circuit."

FREQUENCY OF WORKOUTS

The higher the training intensity, the less frequently you'll need to work out and, in fact, be able to work out. For those of you in the beginner and intermediate categories, three workouts a week, about 48 hours apart, are optimal. For the advanced and the athletes among you using negative training to increase intensity, you may get satisfactory results with two workouts a week. During my Nautilus experience with trainer Ken Hutchins, I was unable to tolerate three intense 18-minute Nautilus workouts a week. After switching to a Monday–Thursday schedule, I found results coming no less quickly but with a great deal more energy and vitality. I've since seen this with scores of other hard workers.

Skeptical of such a small number of workouts a week? There's only one way you'll be convinced—by giving it a try and seeing if it actually works.

THE NEED FOR A WARM-UP

With all the time you're saving by doing one set of reps instead of three or more, you'll have plenty of time to warm up before hopping on the first Nautilus machine. Why bother? Because a proper warm-up, which increases the pliability of muscles and tendons and raises the internal temperature of the body, will both enhance training gains and reduce the risk of injury.

If you've trained aerobically before your strength circuit, there's no need to warm up again. If Nautilus is your first stop in the fitness center, you should devote at least five

INTRODUCTION TO NAUTILUS

minutes to a general, whole-body aerobic warm-up. Just as you would prepare for an aerobic bout, start easy and build gradually. Unlike the aerobic warm-up, though, there's no need to get your heart rate into its target zone. What you're trying to do instead is take as many as possible of the muscles you'll be strength-training, and your connective tissue (tendons primarily), through a nice range of motion. The best pre-Nautilus warm-up choices, therefore, are whole-body activities such as brisk walking or cross-country skiing. Even after a warm-up, though, you'd be safest taking it easy with the first three or four reps of *each* Nautilus machine in your workout.

THE FOURTEEN COMMANDMENTS OF NAUTILUS TRAINING

1. Perform only one set of four to six exercises for the lower body and six to eight for the upper body. Modify this if any of your sport activities involve disproportionate use of the lower body. Compound machines count as two exercises.
2. Select your weight load so that you'll reach failure in about 12–15 reps. If you're just starting out, the first four to six workouts should be done with light weights and not go to failure.
3. Continue each exercise to the point of momentary muscular failure, when no additional reps can be completed in perfect form. If you reach 15 reps in two consecutive workouts, increase the weight 5 to 10 pounds in the following workout.
4. Never rest the weight stack more than a fraction of a second between repetitions.
5. Always work the larger muscles first. Beginning a workout with exercises that train the smaller muscles can fatigue you and reduce possible training gains with the larger muscles.
6. Concentrate on letting each machine draw you

SPORTSPERFORMANCE

slowly into the stretched starting position. If this position is uncomfortable, have a spotter or instructor pin the weight stack to reduce the range of motion.

7. Move more slowly in the negative or lowering phase than in the positive or lifting phase.
8. Move the weights at a speed that can best be described as "slow and controlled." *Never* throw the weights at high speed, or "explode" into them in the vain and dangerous aim of training to increase power.
9. To maximize strength gains, rest between machines. To maximize stamina gains, move rapidly from machine to machine.
10. Always breathe normally. Breath-holding is a frequent cause of fainting, and may induce a coronary incident or stroke because of the resulting increase in blood pressure.
11. Train no more than three times a week, with about 48 hours between workouts. If this proves too much, eliminate the middle workout.
12. Keep accurate records so that you can progress at a constant and measured pace.
13. Vary your workouts at least every nine weeks to avoid plateaus or staleness.
14. Don't forget to call home at least once a week.

INTRODUCTION TO NAUTILUS

MUSCULAR SYSTEM OF THE LEG— ANTERIOR AND POSTERIOR

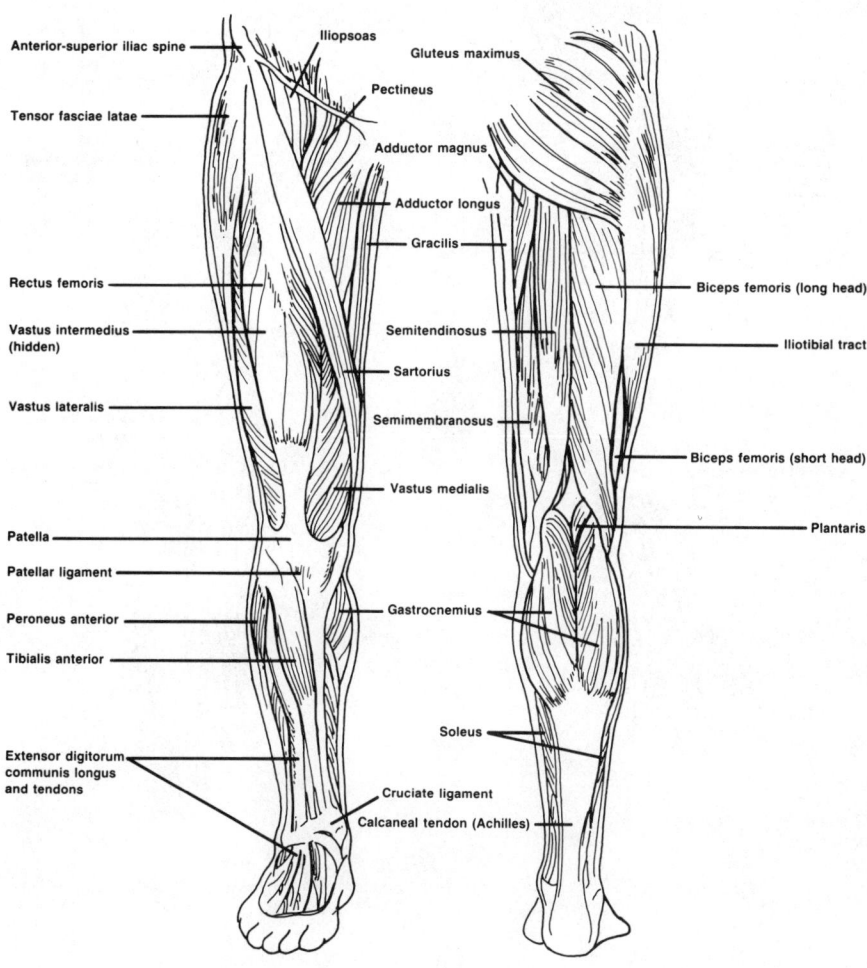

SPORTSPERFORMANCE

MUSCULAR SYSTEM OF THE ARM— ANTERIOR AND POSTERIOR

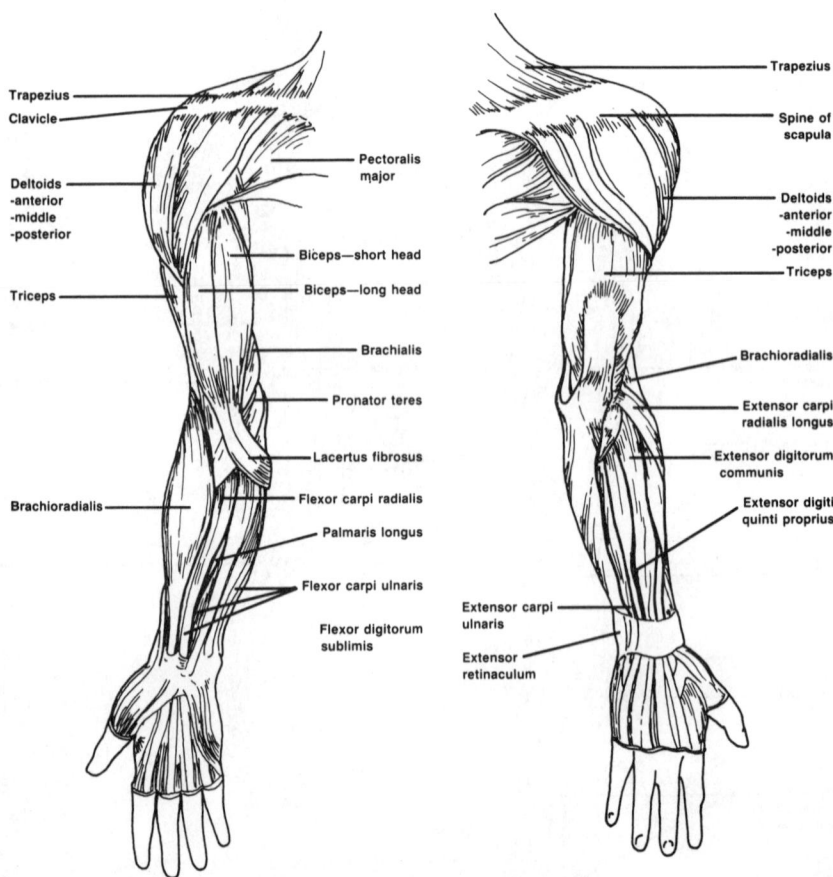

INTRODUCTION TO NAUTILUS

MUSCULAR SYSTEM OF THE TRUNK—POSTERIOR

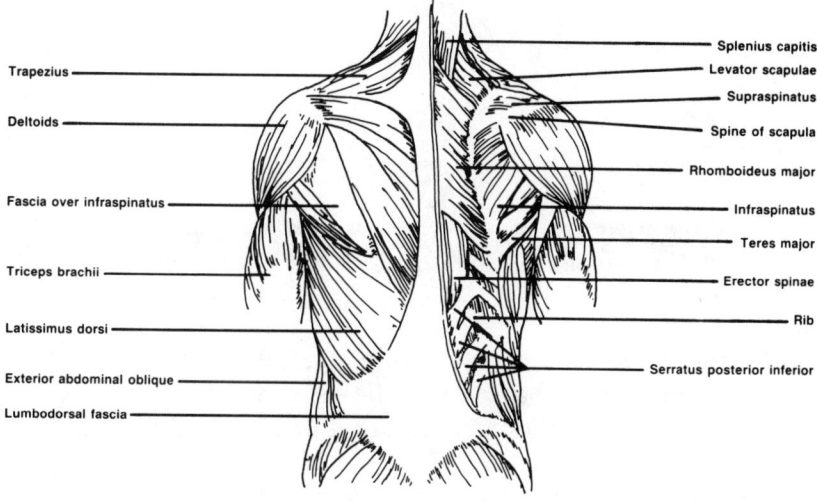

6
THE LOWER BODY

The following four chapters bring you what you've been waiting for. Each chapter will be preceded by a list of muscle groups and the machines that can be used to train them.

Use this book at your fitness center. Don't expect to memorize the training details at home then jump right into a perfect workout at the gym. The correct use of these machines is not always obvious, and results will suffer if you don't start out by doing it right!

Your workouts will generally start with the lower body, since large muscle groups should be trained before small. For variation (see Chapter 10), workouts *can* be started with the upper body.

Okay, here we go:

Muscle Groups	Nautilus® Machine
Hip Extensors Gluteus maximus, hamstrings	Duo Squat, Hip and Back, Leg Curl
Hip Flexors Rectus femoris of the quadriceps group, iliopsoas	Hip Flexor, Leg Extension

LOWER BODY

Muscle Groups	Nautilus® Machines
Quadriceps Vastus lateralis, medialis, intermedius; rectus femoris	Duo Squat, Leg Extension, Compound Leg
Hamstrings Semimembranosus, Semitendinosus, Biceps Femoris	Duo Squat, Leg Curl, Hip and Back
Adductors Adductor longus, brevis; gracilis	Adductor Machine
Abductors Gluteus medius, minimus; Tensor Fascia Latae	Abductor Machine
Ankle Extensors Gastrocnemius; Soleus	Calf Raise (Multi-Exercise)
Ankle Flexors Tibialis Anterior	Foot Flexion (Leg Curl)

THE HIP AND BACK MACHINE

1. Slide onto pad from either side and place both legs over the rollers.
2. Arms are extended, grip open; hip joint should roughly match the cam's rotation axis.

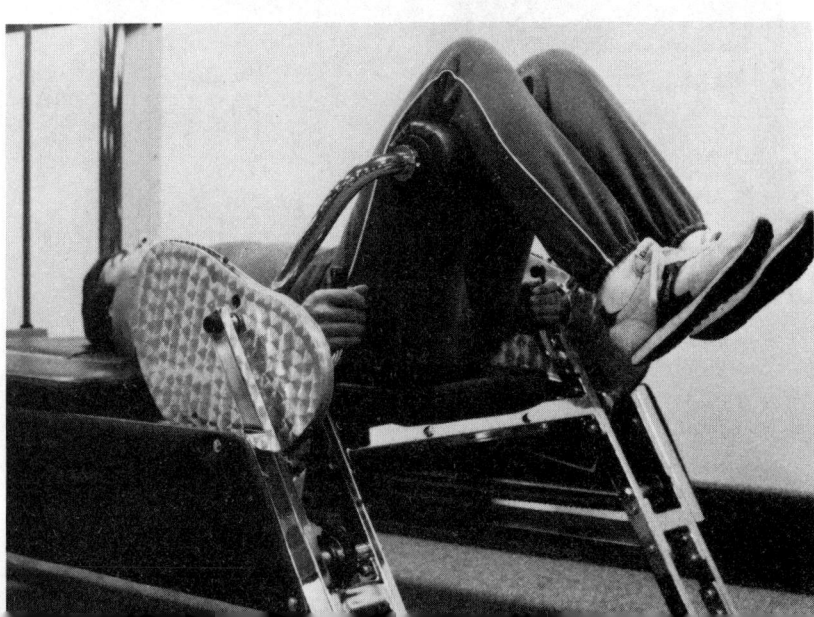

SPORTSPERFORMANCE

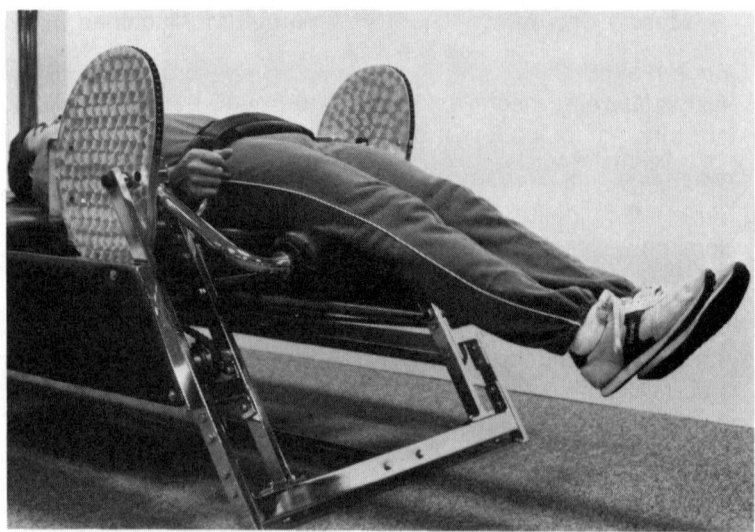

Extend both legs slowly and completely. Do not arch back by extending beyond 180°-190°. Hold this position for a count of two.

1. *Holding one leg perfectly steady, let the other leg rise toward the torso.*
2. *As the leg raises, let the lower leg flex backward to form about a 90° angle with the back of the thigh.*

LOWER BODY

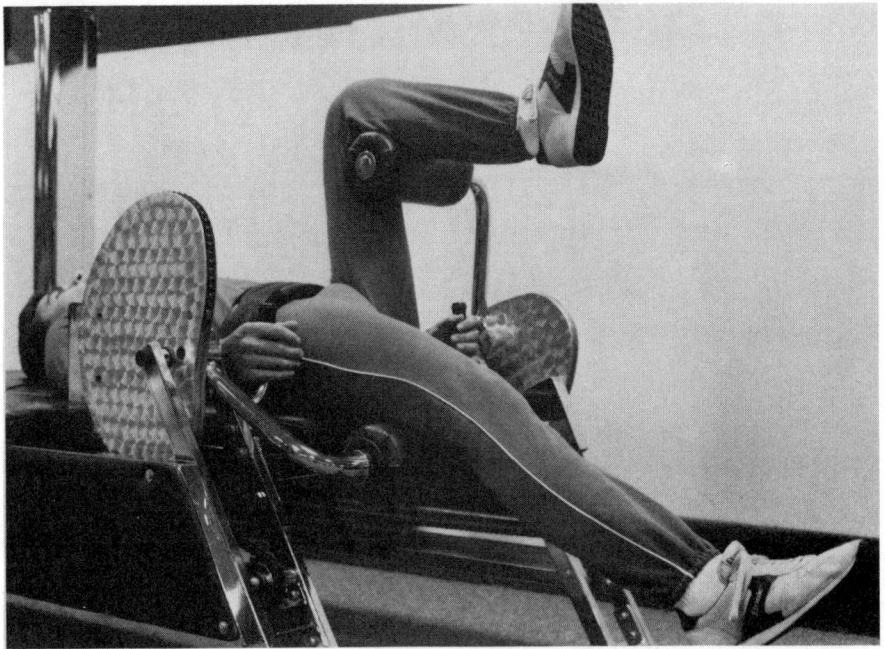

1. At full flexion of the leg on the torso, and keeping the down leg motionless, return the up leg to its starting position.
2. Do not extend the up foot toward the ceiling. Your return to starting position (hip extension) should exactly mimic the hip flexion movement.
3. Pause for a count of two in the fully extended position. Do not arch the back.
4. Repeat with the opposite leg.

SPORTSPERFORMANCE

THE DUO SQUAT MACHINE

1. Seat position can only be set from inside the machine through trial and error.
2. Climb in and push yourself firmly up into the shoulder pads. Maintain an open grip.
3. Place both feet onto the foot pedals at the lowest position.

Push out slowly until you either extend the legs fully or reach the crossbar (next photo). Correct seat position will not allow you to extend the legs fully.

LOWER BODY

1. Locate the crossbar with the two bolts and set your seat position so the machine's levers meet these bolts when your legs are extended to 160°-170°.
2. If you can extend your legs fully before the levers reach the bolts, move the seat closer.

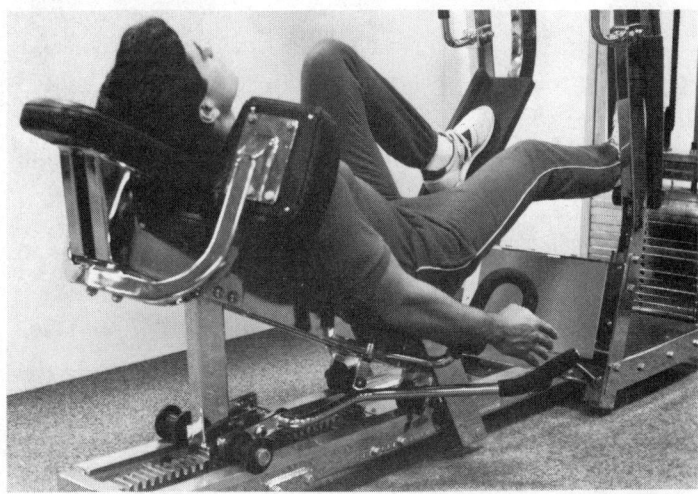

1. Now you're ready to go. With both legs extended, keep one motionless and let the other flex slowly backward toward the torso.
2. Get as full a flexion as possible, then slowly extend outward toward the other leg.
3. Hold this position and repeat with the opposite leg.

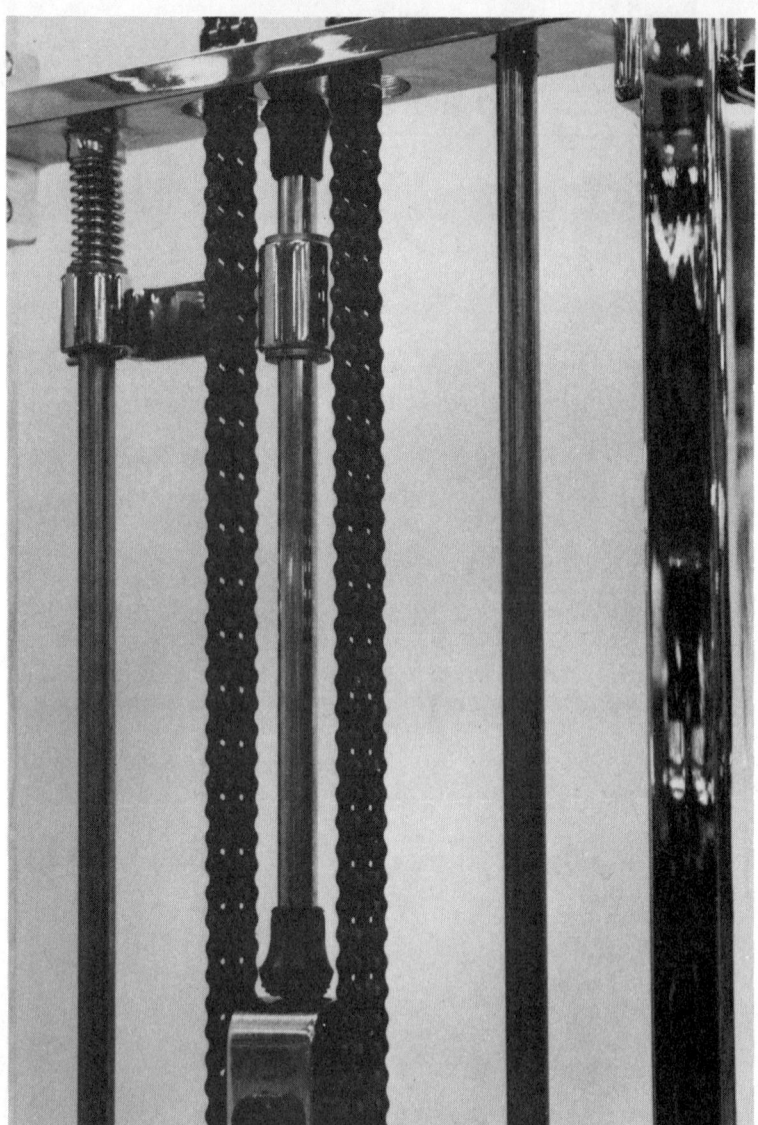

1. The infimetric bar can be swung into position between the chains and above the weight stack.
2. Infimetric or akinetic training requires that you extend both legs simultaneously until the weight stack presses the infimetric bar against the cross-member.
3. Slowly extend one leg while resisting and flexing with the other. Do not let the weight stack drop off the infimetric bar.
4. Reverse movements by extending the flexed leg and resisting with the opposite.
5. Nautilus has arbitrarily called this exercise Infimetric *if you do it with zero or one plate*, and Akinetic *if you use more than one plate*. Don't ask why.

LOWER BODY

THE LEG EXTENSION MACHINE

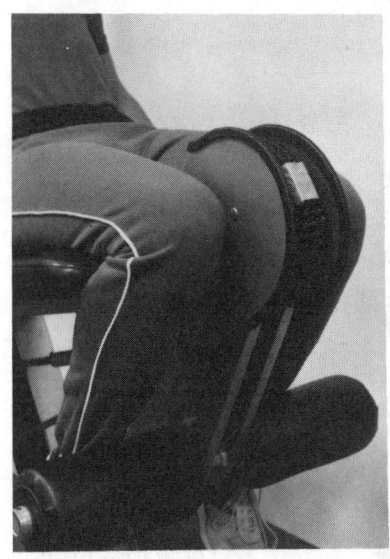

If your machine has an adjustable seat back, position it so that your knees align with the machine's axis of rotation.

On a nonadjustable-seat leg extension, you may require one long back pad to move you forward into the correct position.

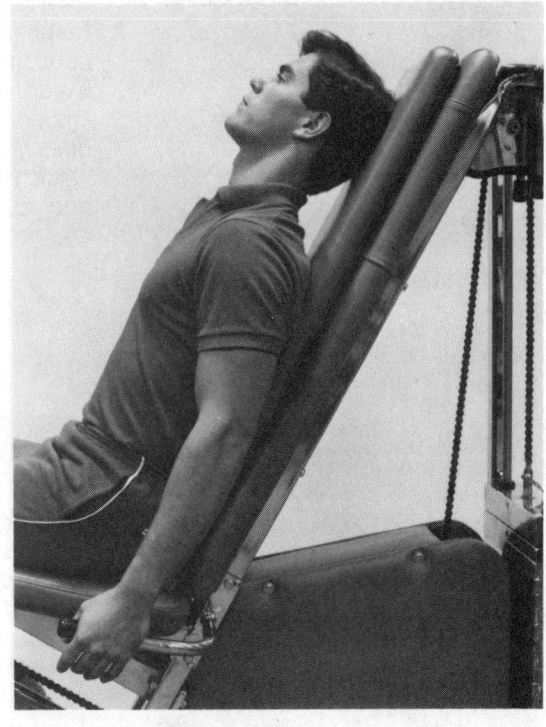

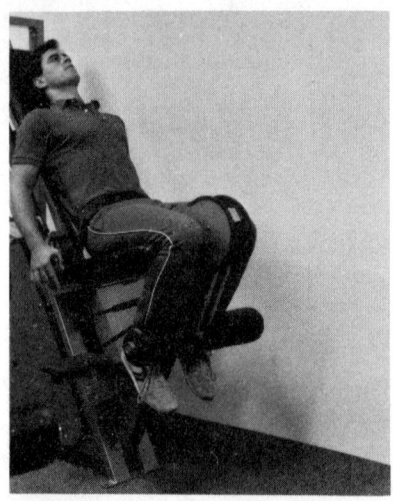

1. You may find it easiest to place your feet behind the rollers before sitting back.
2. With an open grip and the head and torso relaxed against the back pad, assume the starting position.

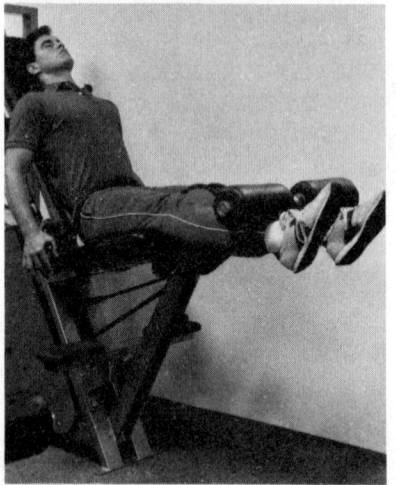

1. Extend both legs slowly to 180° and hold this position for a count of two.
2. Return both legs simultaneously but do not rest the weight stack upon full flexion. If your weight load does reach the rest of the stack, touch down briefly and go. I call this "touch and go."

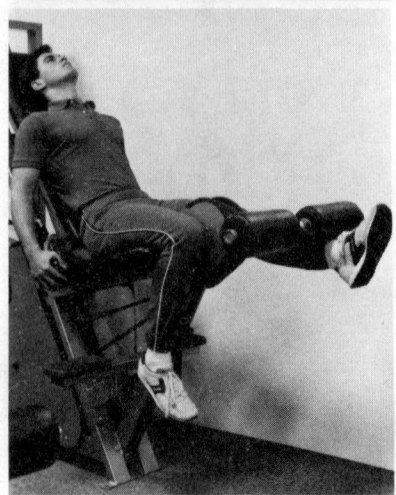

You may do unilateral (one-leg) negatives by extending with both legs then dropping one off and lowering with the other. This is called "negative-accentuated exercise."

LOWER BODY

THE COMPOUND LEG MACHINE

Perform the leg extension exercise as above.

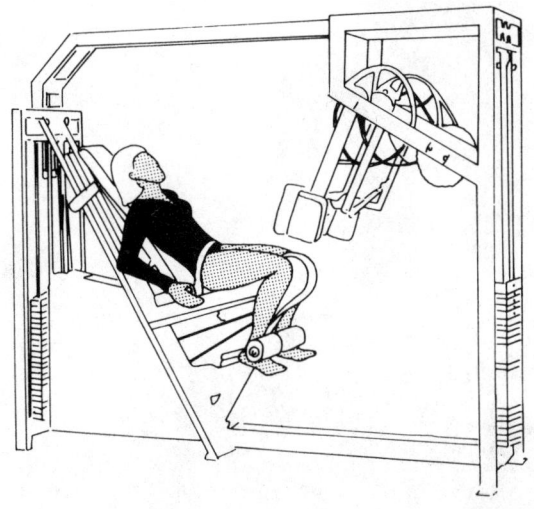

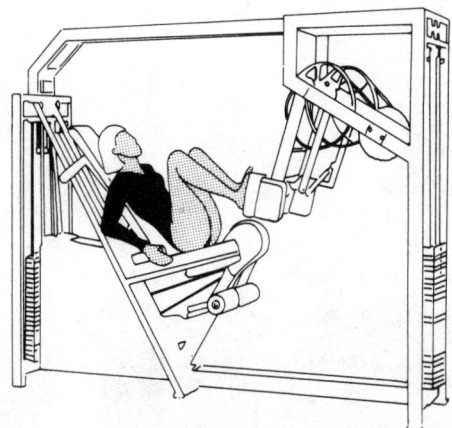

1. Swing the foot pads down into position for the squat.
2. Move the seat forward to give you a more complete range of motion. If you have knee problems, do not move the seat forward.
3. Keeping an open grip and the head and torso back and relaxed, extend out slowly to just short of the 180° position.
4. Hold for a count of two and return slowly.

SPORTSPERFORMANCE

THE LEG CURL MACHINE

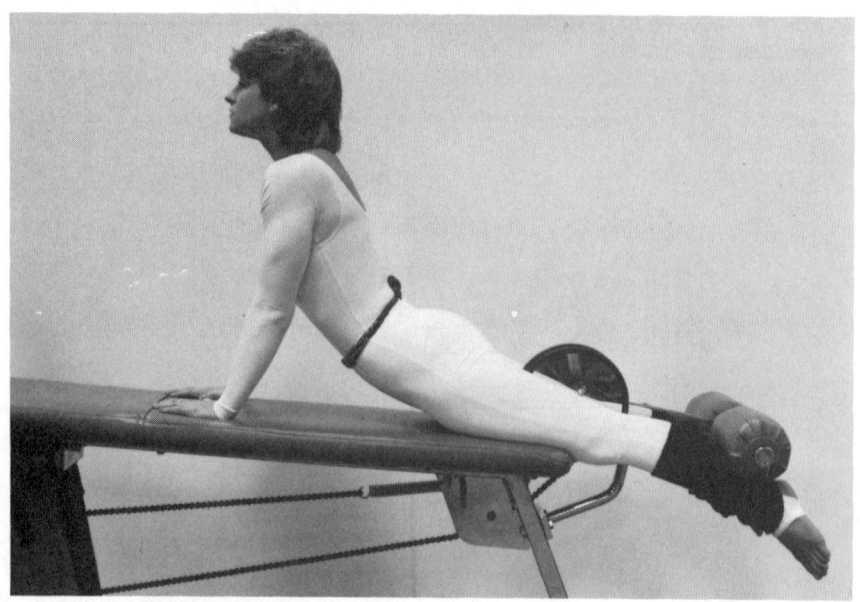

Position feet beneath rollers before lying down on pad. Knees should be just off the pad surface.

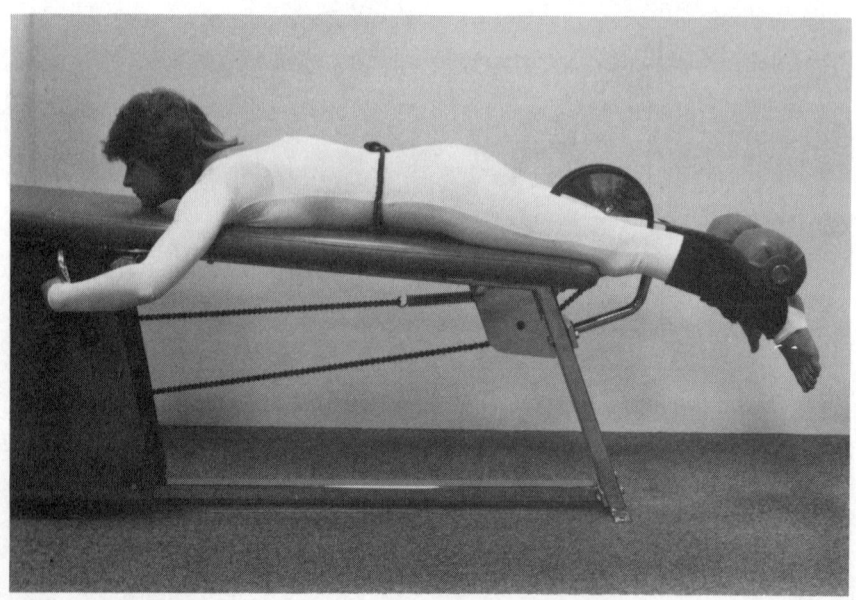

Starting position. Feet are flexed slightly downward.

LOWER BODY

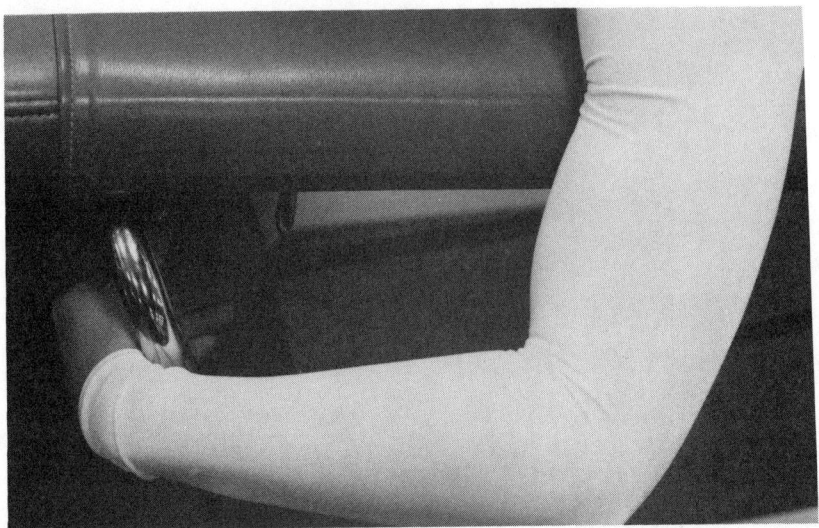

Close-up of grip. Holding with flexed wrists prevents you from squeezing hard enough with your handgrip to dangerously raise blood pressure.

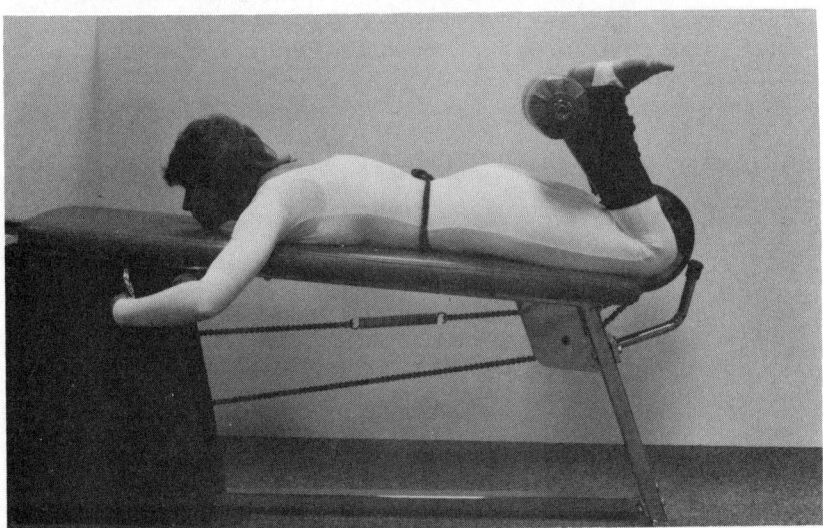

1. Flex slowly upward as far as possible while keeping the hips down.
2. Do not *let your buttocks rise to increase the range of motion. You were simply taught incorrectly if you train that way now. With work you will get the same range of motion, better results, and a healthier back from keeping the hips down.*

SPORTSPERFORMANCE

THE ADDUCTOR MACHINE (AND COMBINATION ADDUCTOR/ABDUCTOR)

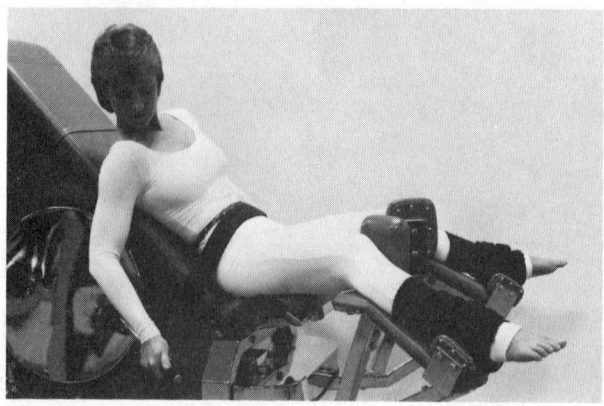

1. Familiarize yourself with the adjustment lever. Pushing it in and turning it counterclockwise will separate the knee pads and increase your range of motion.
2. Through trial and error, set the machine so that your legs are abducted (separated) as widely as possible. The adjustment procedure will be identical on the Combination Ad/Ab machine.

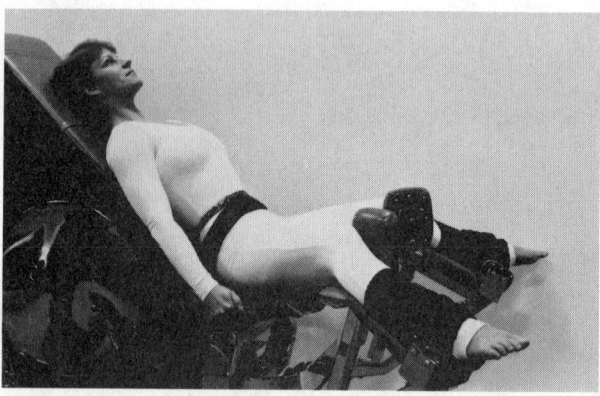

1. With the torso and head back and relaxed, squeeze the legs together. Pressure should be exerted by rolling the knees slightly inward. The feet are along for the ride and do nothing.
2. Squeeze and hold in the fully contracted position for a count of two, then slowly return to the abducted position.

LOWER BODY

THE ABDUCTOR MACHINE

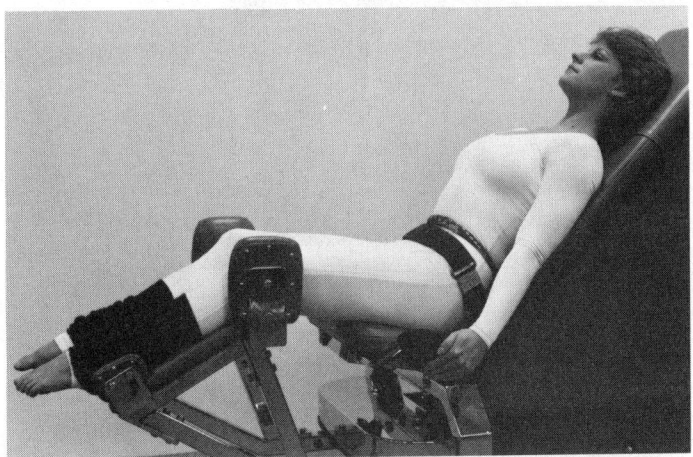

Sit back, relax, and belt in. If your knees do not meet the knee pads (short people only, for the most part), use a full-length back pad behind you.

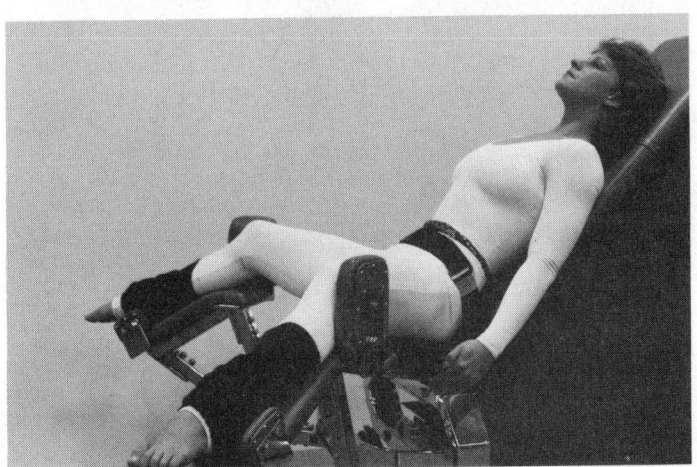

1. Abduct (separate) the legs slowly and as fully as possible. Press with the knees, not the feet.
2. Hold this abducted position for a count of two then return to the adducted starting position. Touch and go—do not rest the weight stack.
3. If you are on the Combination Ad/Ab machine, simply spin the knee pads so that they are outside the knees, then proceed as above.

SPORTSPERFORMANCE

THE MULTI-EXERCISE MACHINE CALF RAISE

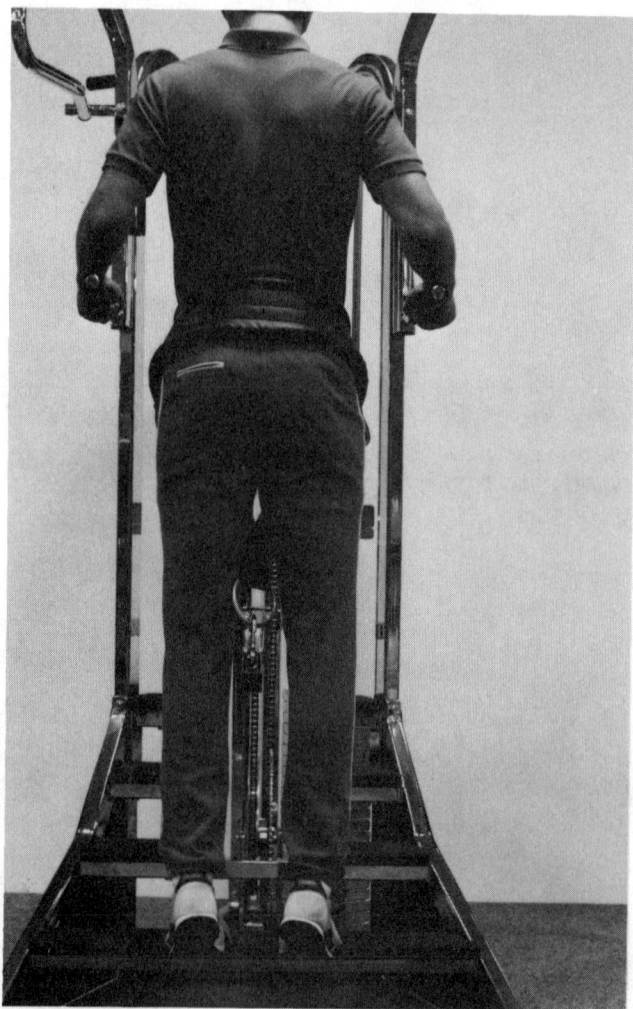

1. Attach the hip belt to the machine's lever.
2. Climb through the belt and position it above your pelvic girdle. It should be in a snug, secure position.
3. Climb to the second step of the platform (new models) or first step (old, adjustable-carriage models).
4. While holding onto the triceps dip bars, raise on your toes as high as possible and hold for a count of two.
5. Lower as fully as possible and repeat.

LOWER BODY

THE LEG-EXTENSION MACHINE FOOT FLEXOR

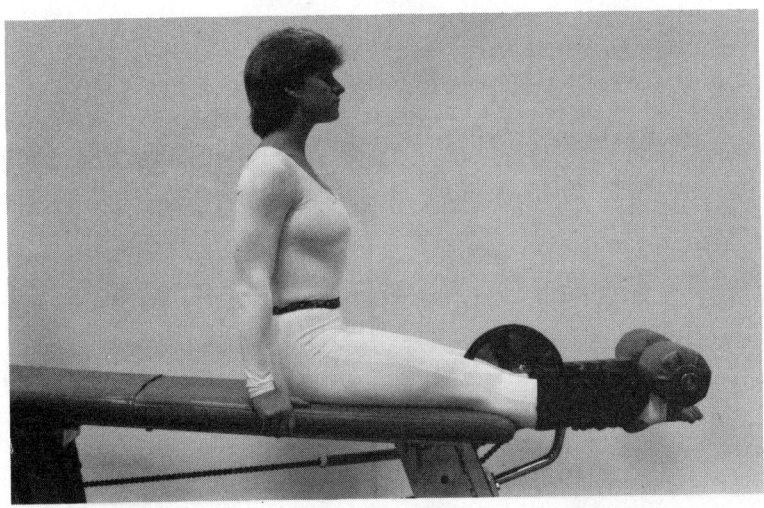

Sit erect and place the feet below the rollers. This exercise can be done with (safest) or without footwear.

1. Dorsiflex the feet (bring toes towards shins) as fully as possible.
2. Move your body backward or forward until you find the position that allows comfortable and full foot movement.

SPORTSPERFORMANCE

THE HIP FLEXOR MACHINE

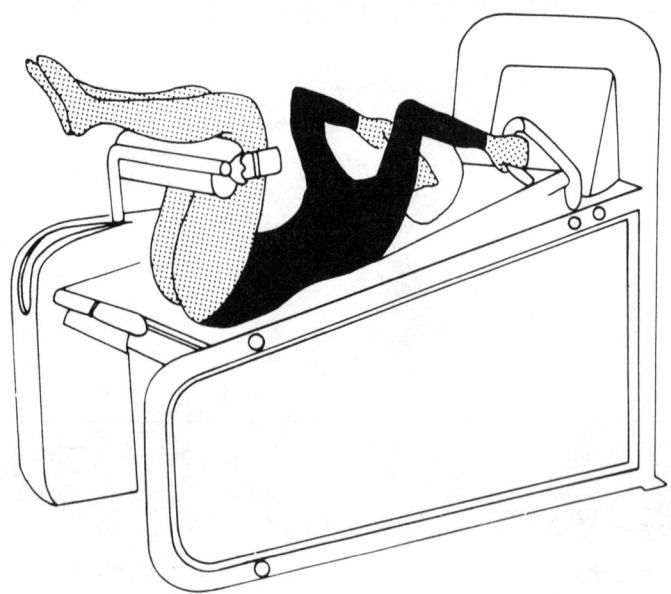

1. Sit and fasten belt across the lower thighs.
2. Lie back and grasp overhead handles with an open grip.
3. Slowly flex your legs toward the torso, pausing for a count of two at full hip flexion. Return slowly and repeat.

7
THE ABDOMEN AND LOWER BACK

THE ABDOMINAL MACHINE

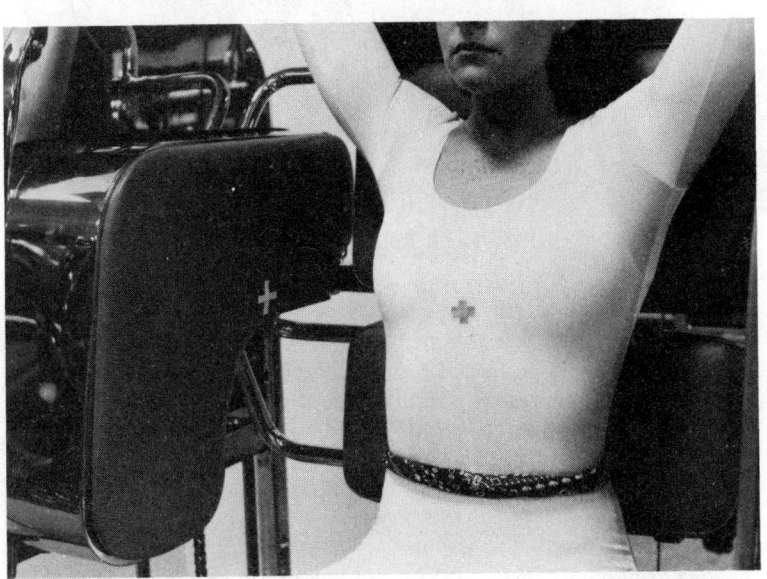

Set seat height so that the tip of your sternum matches the indicated point on the machine.

SPORTSPERFORMANCE

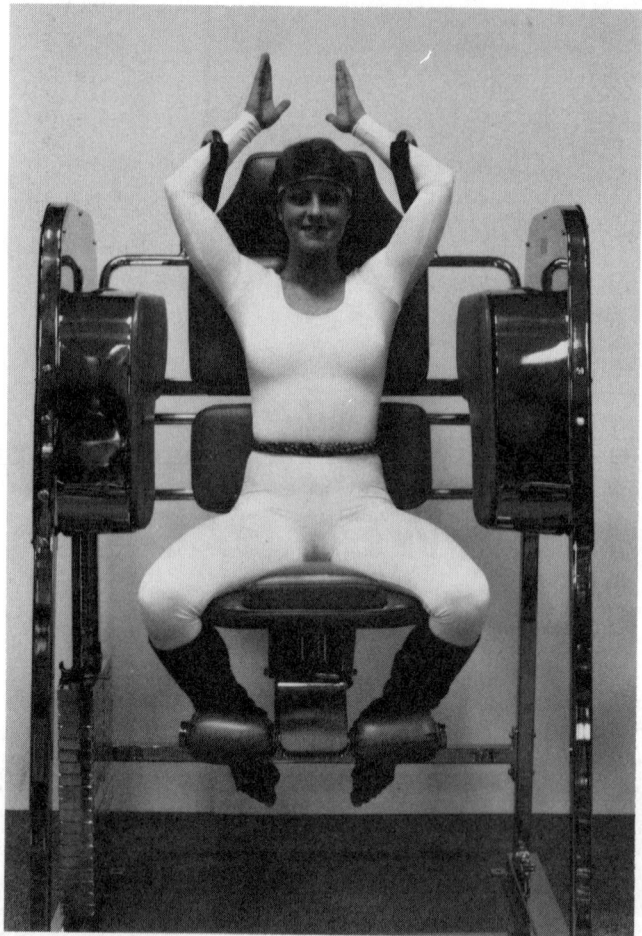

1. Forget about the handgrips—the ones that should never have been put there in the first place. Help isolate your abdominals by threading your lower arms up and through the handles. This will reduce your ability to pull with your arms. (By the way, Nautilus corrected their error here and is now introducing an Abdominal Machine that places resistance against the torso—the way it should have been done the first time.)
2. Forget about the pad on the seat that tells you how widely to separate your legs. It's not too swift either. The wider you can spread your legs, the less the hip flexors can help your abdominals. This is an abdominal machine, not a hip flexor/upper body machine!

ABDOMEN AND LOWER BACK

1. Contract with your abdominals only. This is an extremely difficult machine when done correctly, even with only one plate. If you cannot create enough force with your abdominals alone, add some assistance from the legs, arms, or both.
2. Do not contract through the full range of the machine's motion (another design mistake). Your rectus abdominus only works through one-third to one-half the range of machine travel. After that you must bring in the hip flexors and torso. Go halfway, hold for two, then return. Touch and go with the weight stack.

SPORTSPERFORMANCE

THE ROTARY TORSO MACHINE

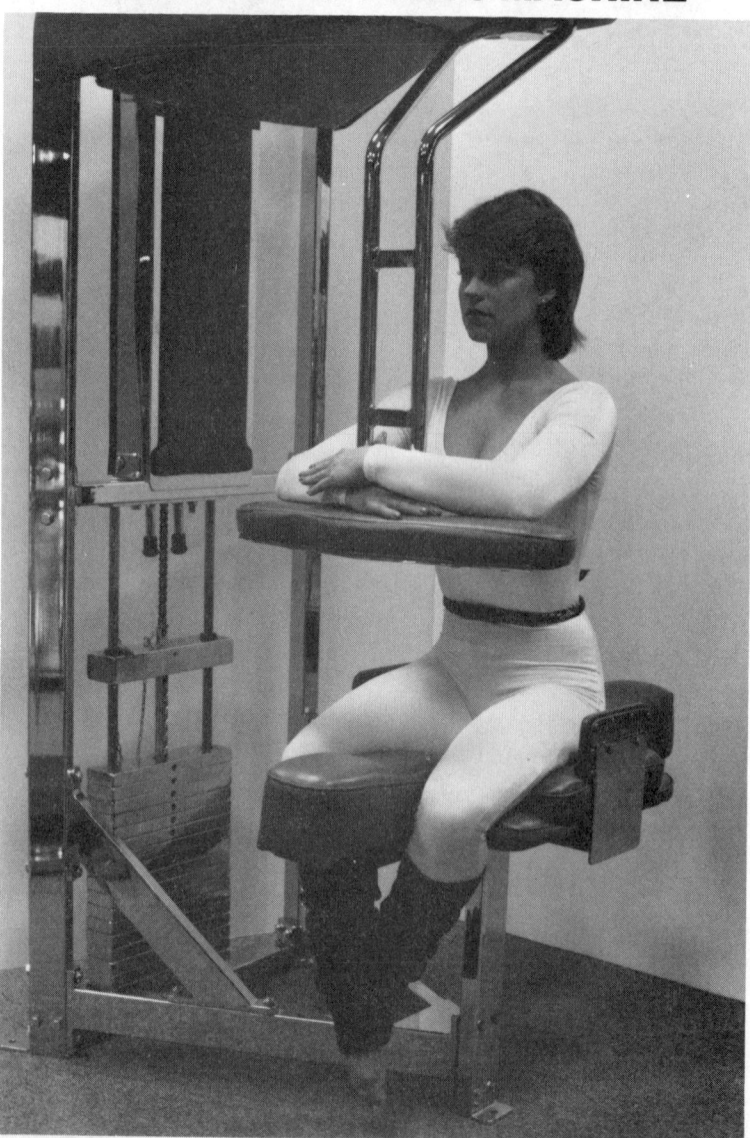

Sit upright and cross arms, gripping with the thumbs only. Begin by facing straight ahead. Your nose should be centered between the two vertical bars, and should never leave this position.

ABDOMEN AND LOWER BACK

 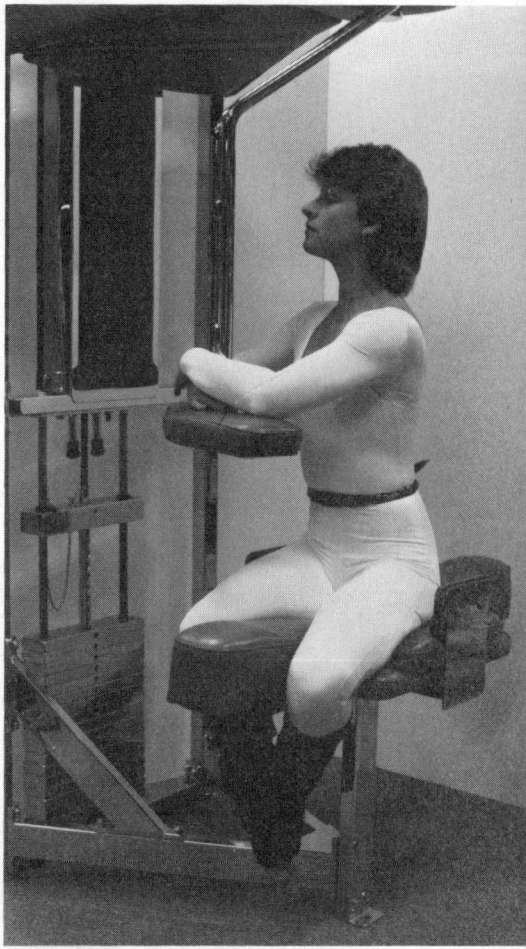

Relax and rotate away from the weight stack into the stretched, starting position. Do not let your gaze stray from between the two bars.

1. Contract and rotate toward the stack. Keep your back as straight as possible and your gaze fixed. This is not an arm exercise, so don't use any muscles but your obliques (and transverse abdominus).
2. Do a full set of reps on one side then turn and repeat for the other.

SPORTSPERFORMANCE

THE LOWER BACK MACHINE

> This machine should absolutely not be used by anyone with back pain, a past history of back pain, or numbness/tingling sensations in the lower body *without* express medical, chiropractic, or osteopathic permission. It is a potentially dangerous machine, and should be used only if you have a completely symptom-free back (or have been cleared). Many back conditions can be worsened by use of this machine.

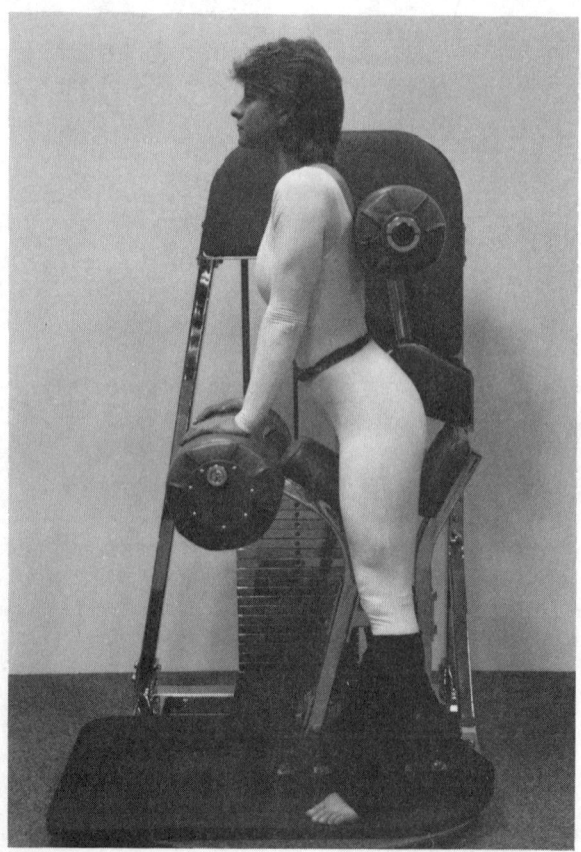

Place one leg over the seat and straddle the machine.

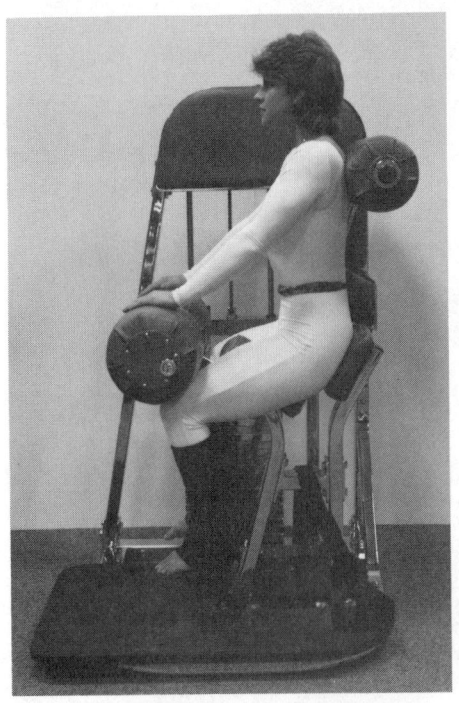

Sit and find a comfortable and stable position for your feet. Rotate the large thigh pads and try placing your feet either on the step or on the base.

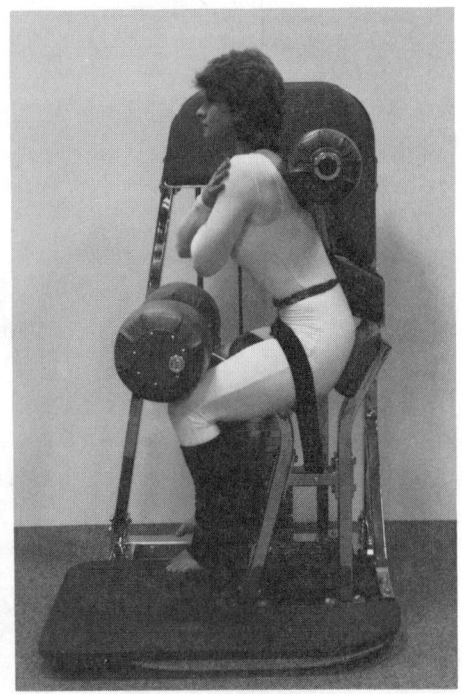

Belt in, cross arms, and lean forward slowly until the weight stack touches down.

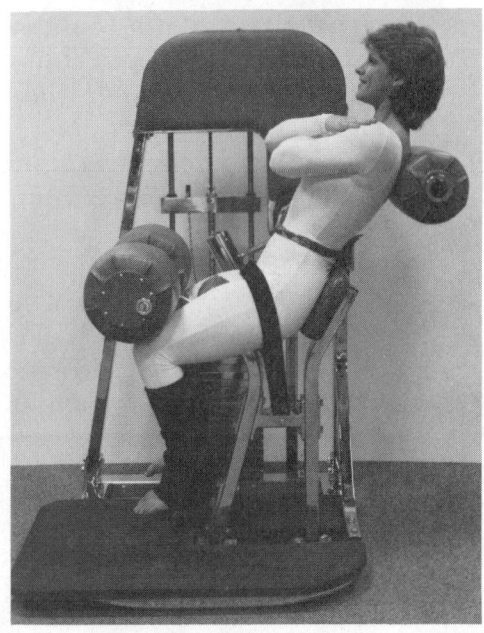

Contract and lean back slowly, going no further than a flat back position. Do not hyperextend the back. Hold for a count of two then return and repeat.

8
THE TORSO AND SHOULDERS

Our focus here is on the three major muscles/muscle groups of the upper body.

Latissimus Dorsi/Teres Major. With the torso fixed they bring the arms down (pulldown exercise); with the arms fixed they raise the torso (chin-ups).

Pectoralis Major and Minor. They bring the arms toward the midline of the chest in several ways (arm cross or pectoral flye exercise; bench press/incline press exercise).

Deltoids (anterior or front, middle, and posterior or rear). They elevate the arms either to the front, side, or overhead (the latter with help from the triceps).

You should expect to devote about half your workout time to these major or "prime" movers—about two exercises or machines for each. Their importance to both daily living and athletic success cannot be over estimated.

Muscles	Nautilus® Machines
Latissimus/Teres Major	Pullover, Pullover/Torso Arm, Behind Neck, Behind Neck/Torso Arm, Torso Arm (freestanding), Multi-Exercise Chin-Ups

TORSO AND SHOULDERS

Muscles	Nautilus® Machines
Pectoralis Major/Minor	Double Chest, Women's Chest, 10° Chest, 40° Chest/Shoulder
Deltoids	Double Shoulder, Lateral Raise (freestanding), Overhead Press (freestanding), 70° Shoulder, 40° Chest/Shoulder, Multi-Exercise Upright Rowing (see Chapter 9), Rowing Torso (rear deltoid only)
Trapezius/Rhomboids	Rowing Torso, Neck and Shoulder
Neck	Four-Way Neck, Rotary Neck, Neck and Shoulder

THE PULLOVER MACHINE

Set seat height so that the axis of cam rotation (cross on padding) aligns with the approximate axis of shoulder rotation. This point will be about an inch below the top of your deltoids.

SPORTSPERFORMANCE

1. Press the foot lever downward to bring the crossbar into position.
2. Grasp the crossbar with one hand to bring it comfortably forward.

1. Place elbows in the pads and the hands alongside the crossbar. Do not grasp the crossbar with a closed grip.
2. Keep feet on lever until correct position is attained. Sit against back pad and make sure belt is secure.

TORSO AND SHOULDERS

1. Remove feet from the lever.
2. Let machine slowly draw you backward into the stretched position.
3. When first learning the use of the machine, use light weight—you don't want to be forced too far backward by a heavy weight stack. The foot lever can always be used to catch the stack if you're in trouble.

1. Slowly bring the crossbar over and down to your abdomen or thighs.
2. Notice the open grip. The movement is performed completely *through pressure from the elbows.* Do not pull the crossbar with your hands (which would greatly reduce latissimus involvement).
3. Pause for a count of two, then return slowly to a full but completely pain-free stretch.

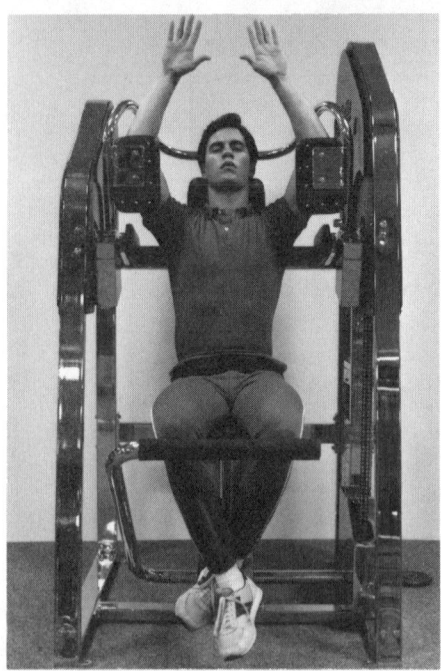

Variation: For even greater latissimus isolation, try using the surface of your upper arms against the elbow pads. This will prevent you quite successfully from using your hands!

1. Near-finishing position on pullover variation.
2. Get as complete a range of motion as possible, but stay pain-free in the stretched position.

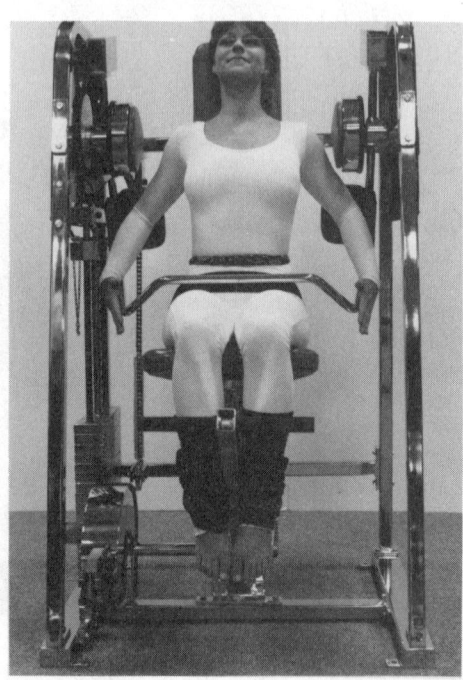

The Women's Pullover: Follow the same instructions as for the men's unit.

TORSO AND SHOULDERS

THE PULLOVER/TORSO ARM MACHINE

Following completion of the Pullover exercise, remove seat belt and reach up to grab Torso Arm bar with palms facing your body. If a spotter or trainer is available, stay belted and have him/her hand you the bar.

1. Pull bar slowly down to chest. Get as full a range of movement as possible.
2. If you cannot fully extend your arms in the starting position, lower the seat as necessary.

SPORTSPERFORMANCE

THE BEHIND NECK/TORSO ARM MACHINE

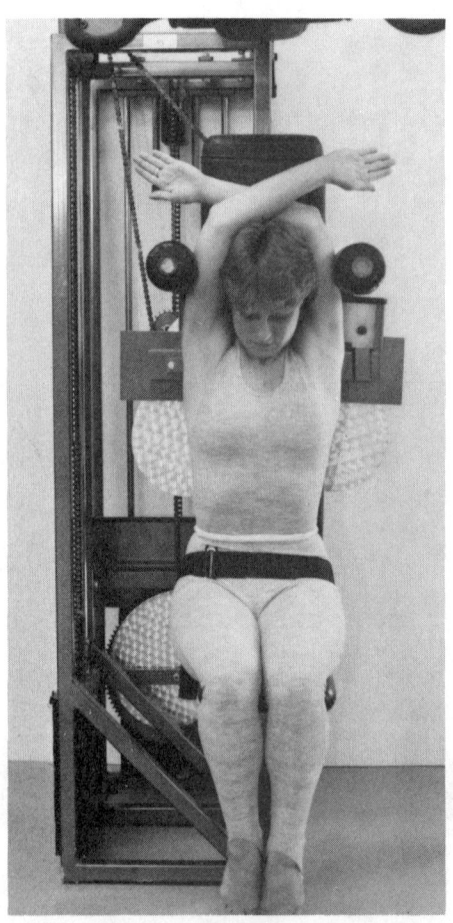
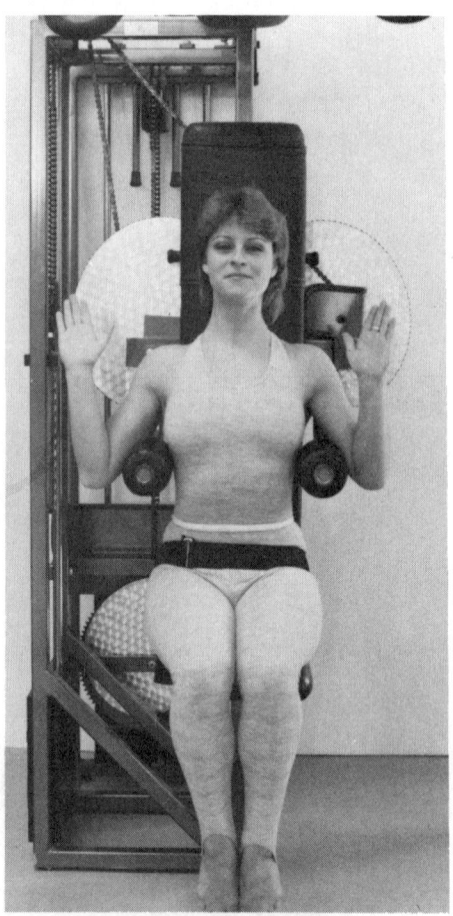

1. Set seat height so that the axis of shoulder rotation (see Pullover) matches the axis of cam rotation.
2. Place arms inside rollers and assume starting position: head is tilted slightly forward to allow arms to cross behind. Palms face directly forward.

1. Squeeze downward while keeping palms facing forward and fingers pointing directly at ceiling.
2. Hold rollers against sides for a count of two then return to starting position and repeat.

TORSO AND SHOULDERS

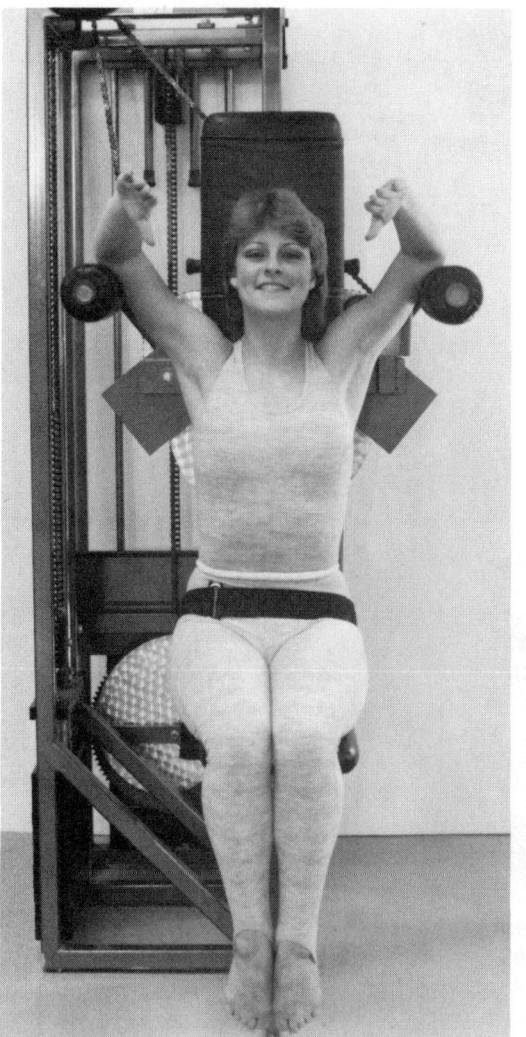

For a variation, have arms facing forward and exert pressure with inside of the upper arm/elbow.

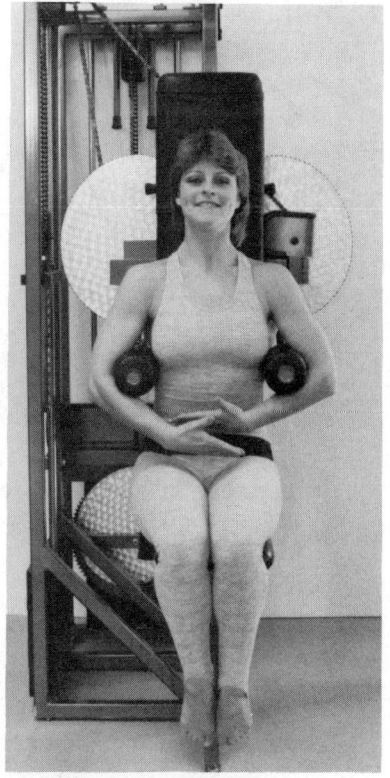

Finishing position. Squeeze rollers, hold for two, return and repeat.

SPORTSPERFORMANCE

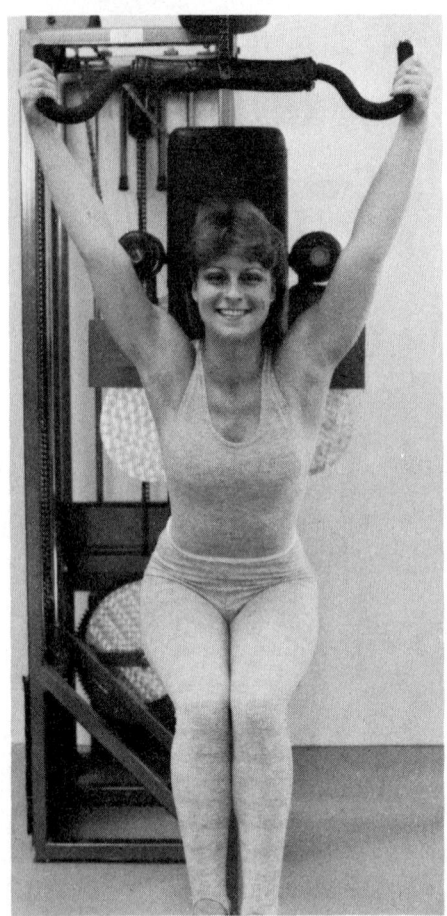

Lean forward. Bring the bar down to the neck or upper shoulders. Hold for a count of two then return.

The Torso Arm Exercise: You may need to remove the seat belt to reach the bar. Shown here is the first of two possible handgrips.

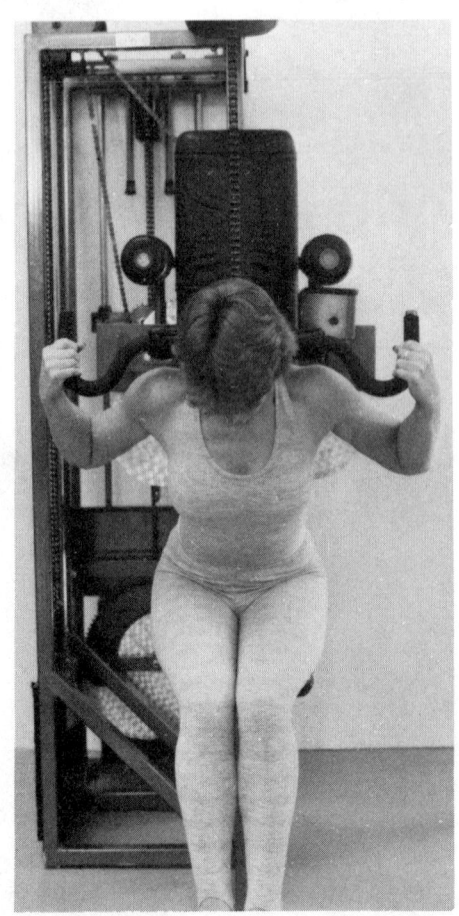

TORSO AND SHOULDERS

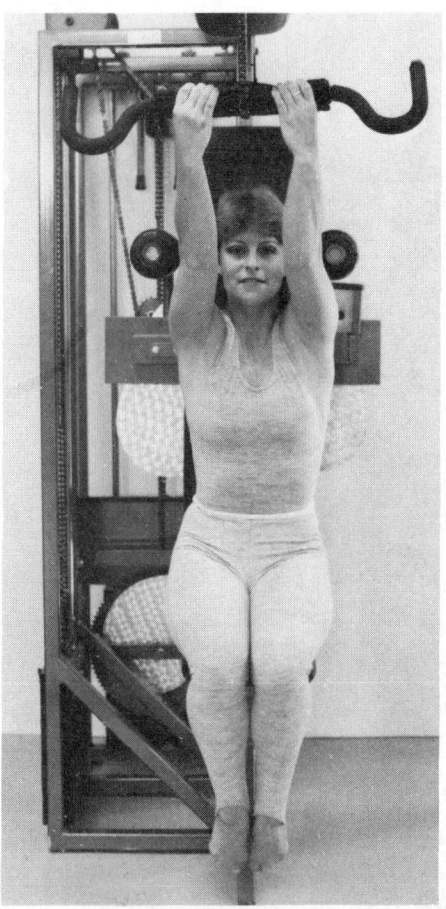

You may have to adjust seat height to get the longest possible range of motion. As always, pause for two at full contraction then return slowly and repeat.

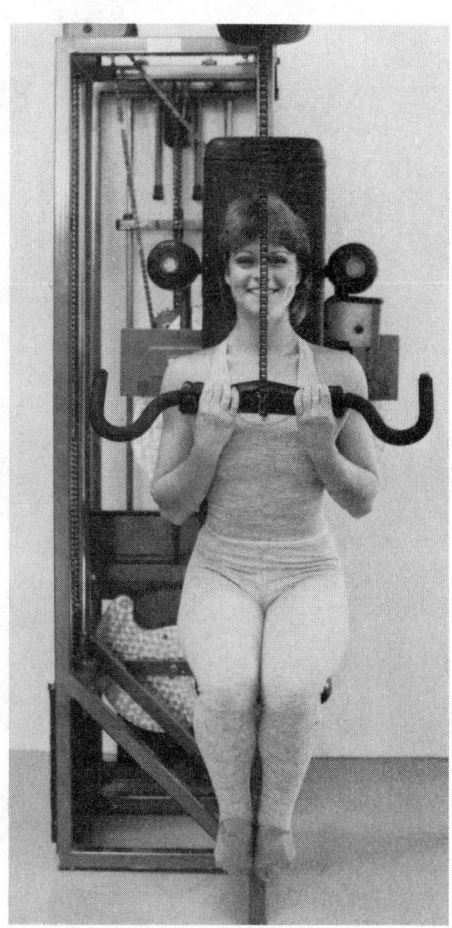

Alternate hand grip. This will place slightly greater stress on the elbow flexors (biceps and brachialis).

SPORTSPERFORMANCE

THE TORSO ARM MACHINE

Starting position, palms facing inward. Seat height is set so that arms can be fully extended.

TORSO AND SHOULDERS

Finishing position. Hold bar on neck for a count of two then return slowly and repeat.

Biceps-emphasizing grip. Follow instructions as above.

SPORTSPERFORMANCE

MULTI-EXERCISE MACHINE CHIN-UPS

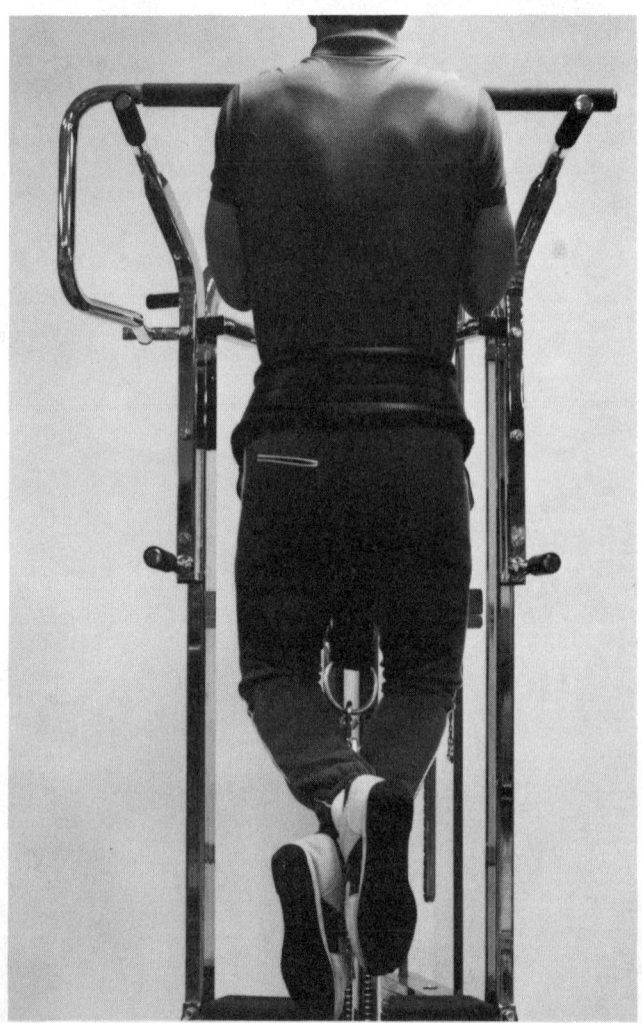

1. Chins can be done with the hip belt to add to your body weight or without.
2. On older models of the Multi-Exercise, adjust the carriage by lifting the two levers. Your chin should be just above the chinning bar when you climb to the top step.
3. On the new, nonadjustable models, use the appropriate step or pull yourself up into the over-the-bar position.
4. Flex legs and cross ankles.

TORSO AND SHOULDERS

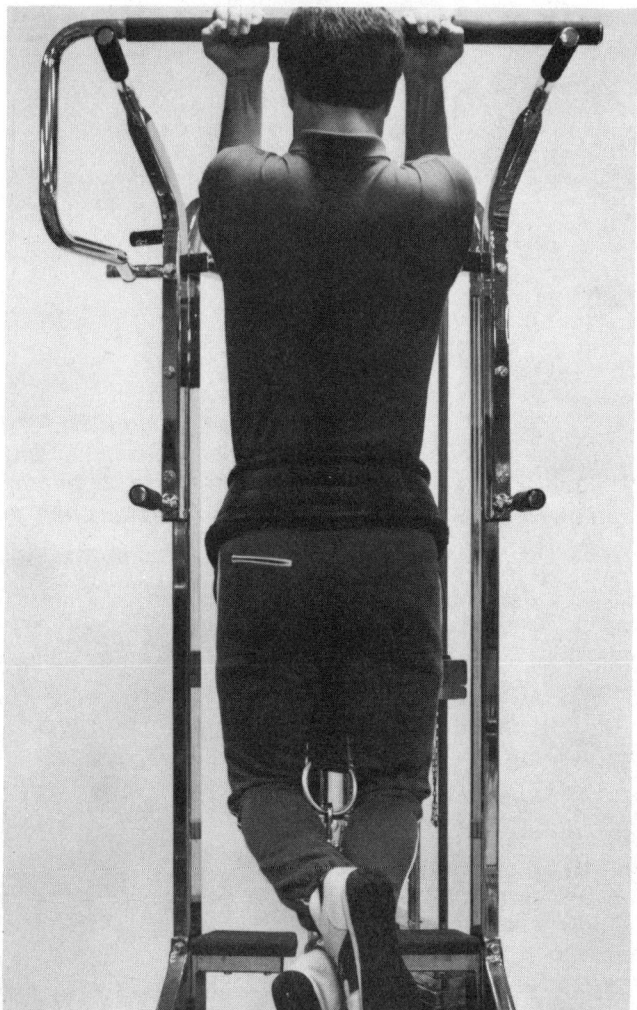

1. With hands about shoulder-width apart, lower yourself slowly into the fully extended position.
2. If you can perform at least five full positive and negative chins (lowering then lifting into starting position), you may use negative-only chins as a bonus. If you cannot do five chins, perform negative-only chins for at least nine workouts.
3. Negative-only: Lower to a count of ten then climb back up steps and repeat. Shoot for at least six negative chins; rest sufficiently between each to make this a more easily reached goal.

SPORTSPERFORMANCE

THE DOUBLE CHEST MACHINE

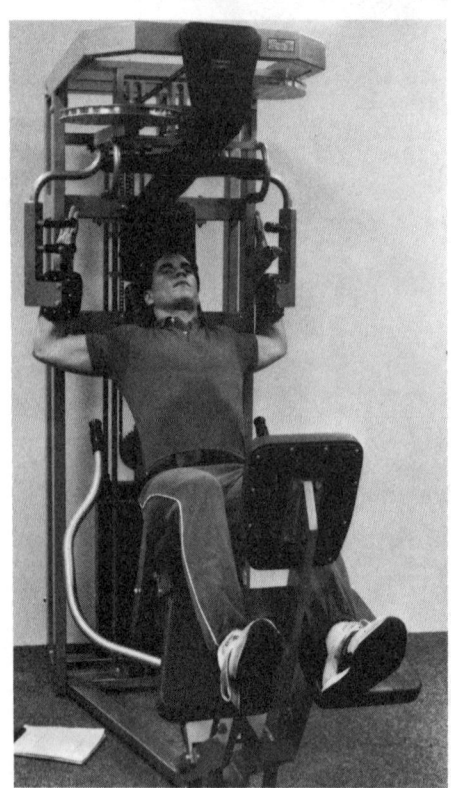

Midposition. Note the 90° angles between upper and lower arms and upper arm and torso, and the open grips.

1. The Arm Cross exercise: Seat height is set so that the upper arms form a 90° angle with the torso.
2. Keep head and back relaxed against pad.
3. Pressure is exerted by the forearms. Do not use a closed grip. Keep your thumbs hooked underneath the grips and your fingers back.
4. Get a full stretch in the starting position.

TORSO AND SHOULDERS

1. Finishing position. Pressure is still being exerted by the forearms. Elbows are directly below the hands. Do not let the elbows flare out to the sides—this reduces pectoralis isolation.
2. Squeeze and hold for a count of two then return to the fully stretched, starting position.

One-arm variation. Grasp overhead grip with one hand then squeeze and hold with other arm for a count of two then return to the fully stretched, starting position.

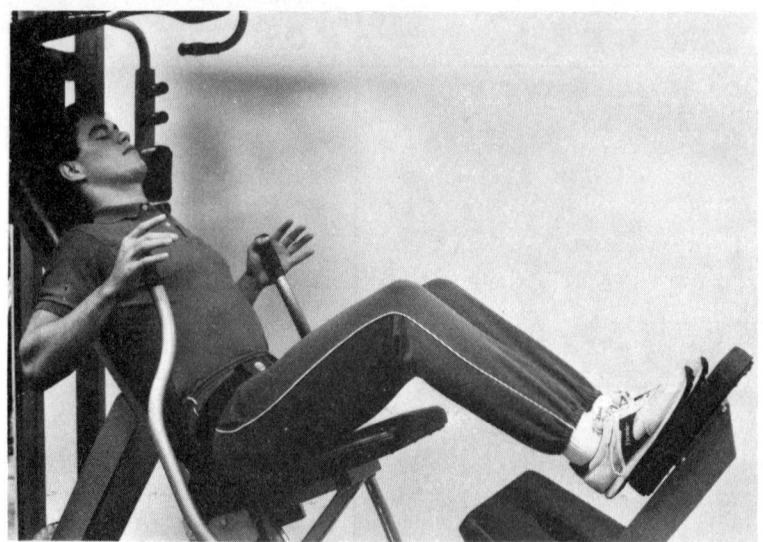

1. The Incline Press exercise. Bring levers into position by pressing out with the feet.
2. Palms may face each other or grasp from above (see next photo).

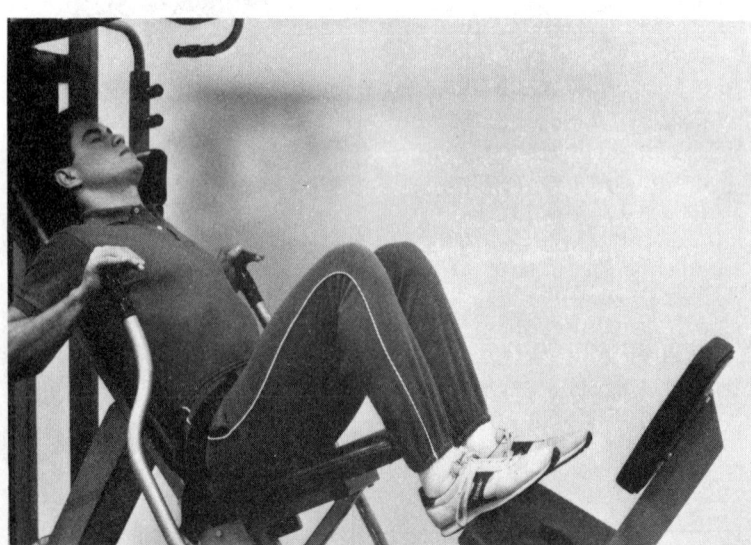

1. Hands are in typical barbell grip position, but not tightly closed around handles. This is starting position.
2. Feet may be rested in this manner to take stress off the lower back. (Try this with the Arm Cross exercise as well.)

Finishing position, barbell grip. Do not go to full extension, where you can (a) rest by locking out and (b) damage your elbow joint by moving too quickly.

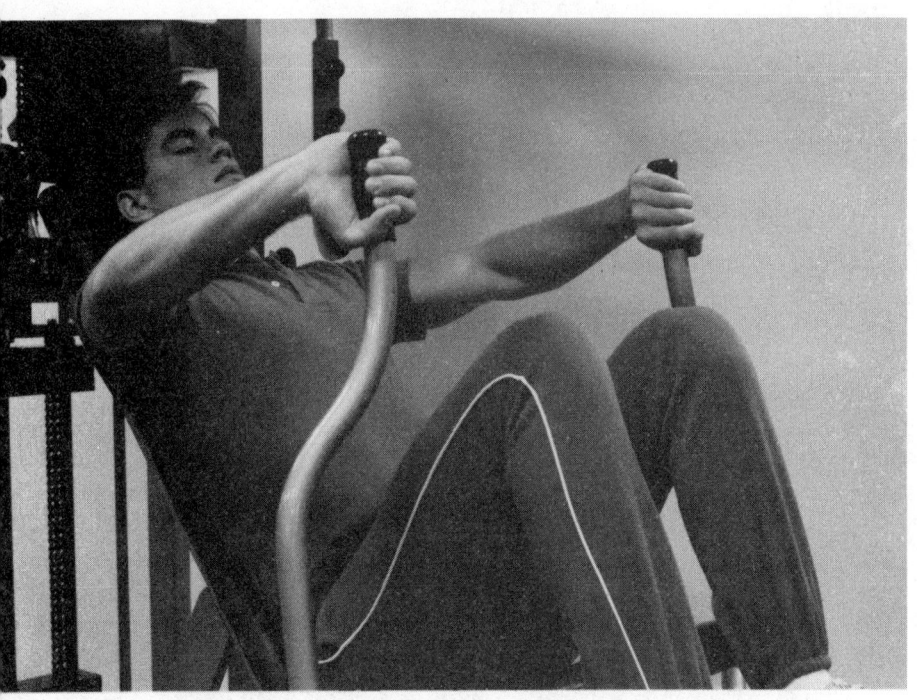

Reverse grip position. Use less weight! This is also a great forearm exercise.

SPORTSPERFORMANCE

For negative-emphasized exercise, a trainer may add to the weight stack's downward pull by squatting up against the foot pedal. This is obviously an advanced variation and must be done carefully.

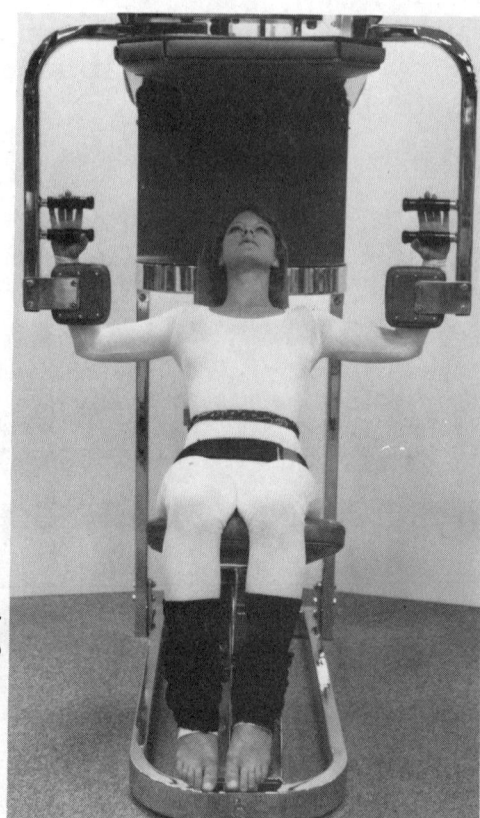

The Women's Chest Machine: Follow instructions as for the Arm Cross exercise.

TORSO AND SHOULDERS

THE DOUBLE SHOULDER MACHINE

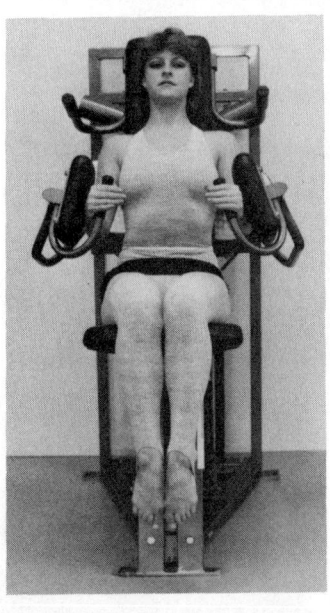

Left:
1. The Lateral Raise: Set seat height so the axis of shoulder rotation (see Pullover) matches the axis of cam rotation.
2. Keep an open grip and lead with the elbows.

Below:
1. Finishing position. Go no higher than a 90° angle between upper arm and torso. Lower arms are parallel to the floor.
2. Keep head and shoulders back and relaxed. Do not let your shoulders "hunch up" or shrug during the exercise.

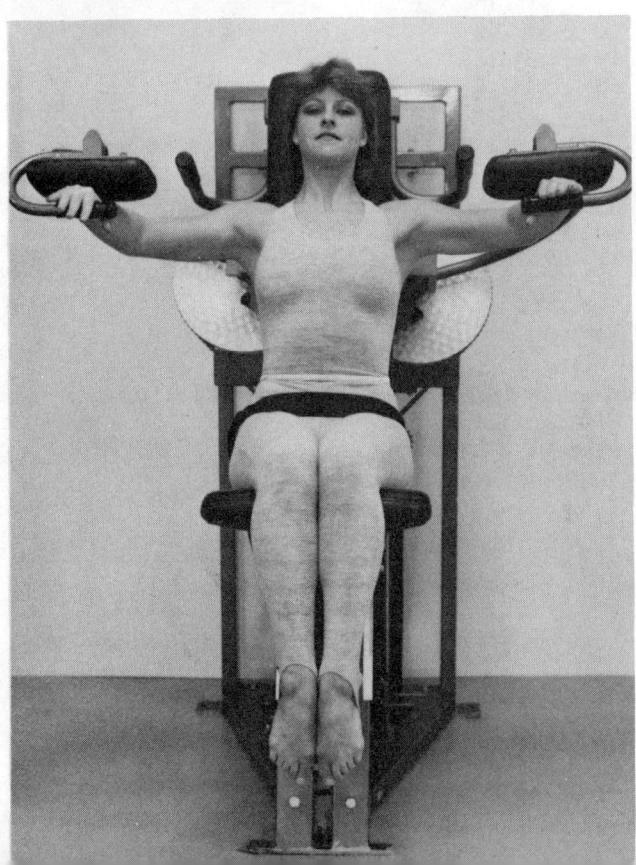

SPORTSPERFORMANCE

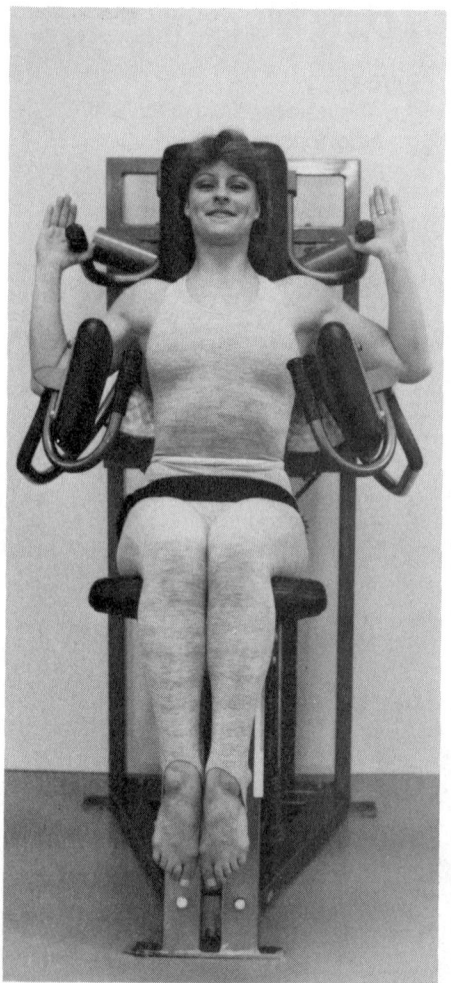

The Overhead Press: Again note the open grip. If the seat is raised you will get a longer range of motion, so don't be afraid to unbelt and climb out of the machine briefly.

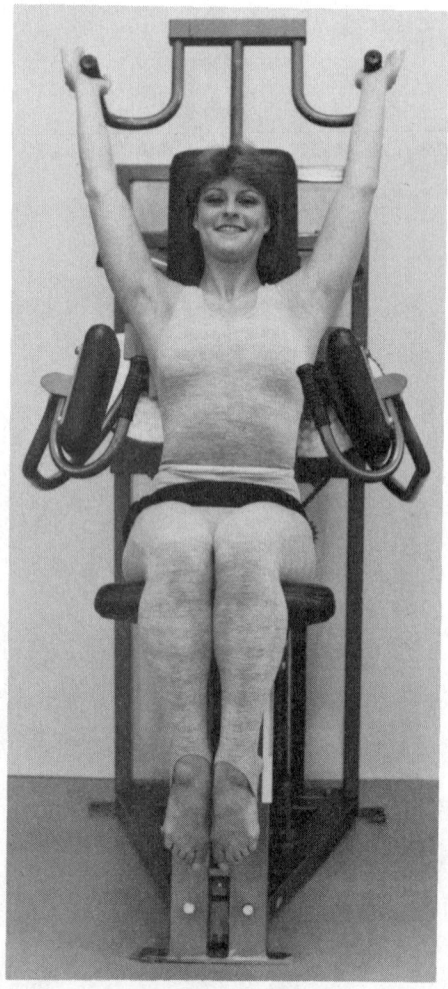

Finishing position. Extend the arms to just short of the lockout position.

TORSO AND SHOULDERS

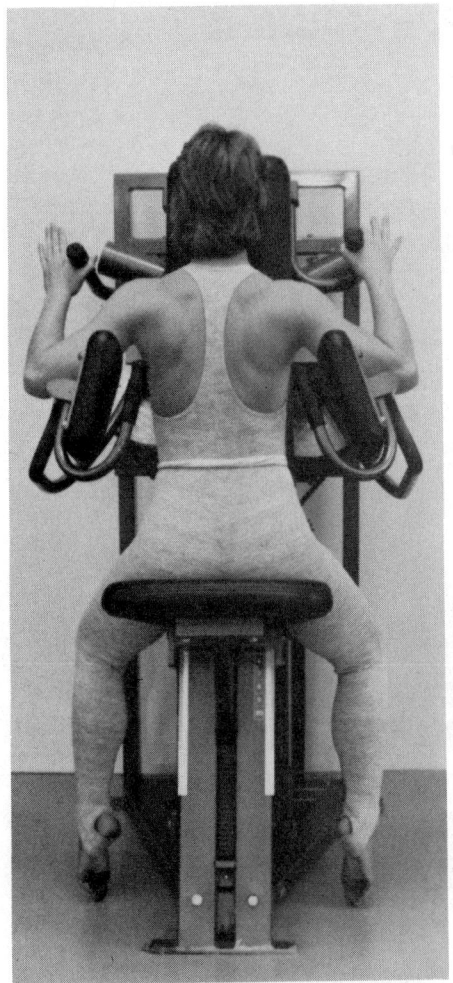

Many people find the standard overhead press position painful to the shoulder. Turning and facing the back pad seems to reduce stress and eliminate the problem.

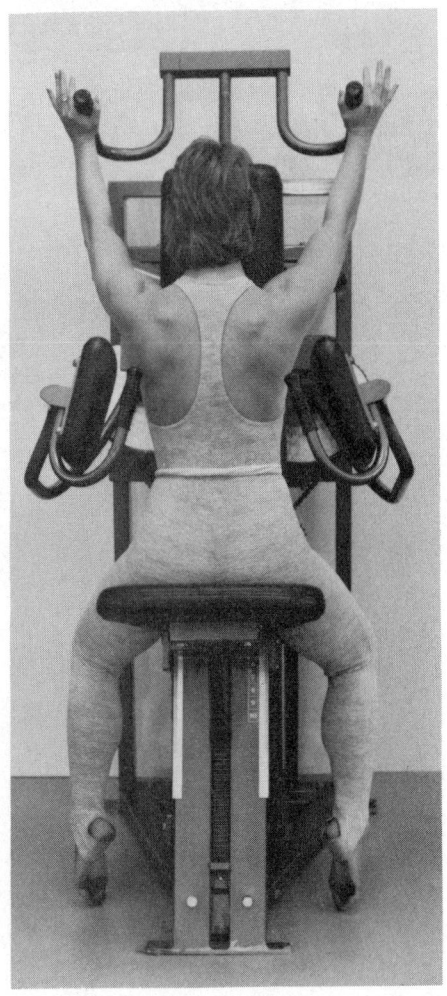

Finishing position. Note open grip and arms just short of lockout.

SPORTSPERFORMANCE

LATERAL RAISE MACHINE

A new machine which does not include the overhead press. Redesign of the arm pads has improved on the original model. Instructions for use, however, are identical.

Finishing position.

TORSO AND SHOULDERS

70° SHOULDER MACHINE

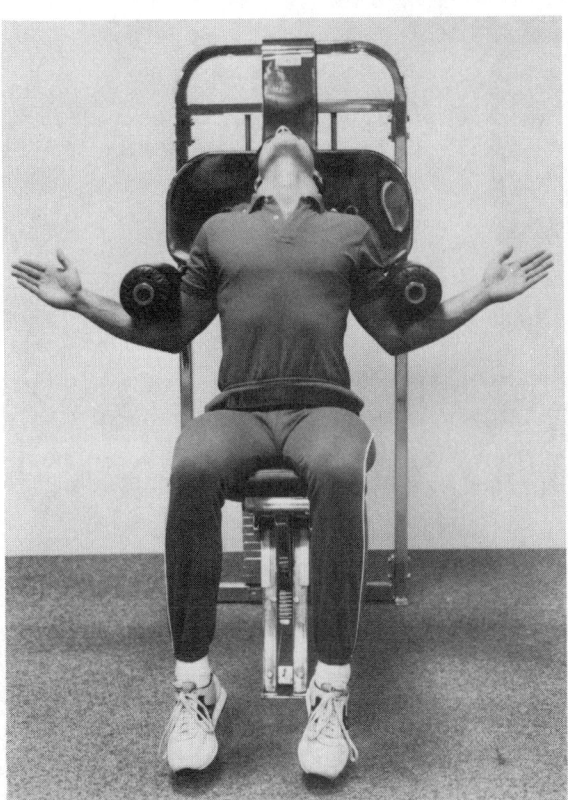

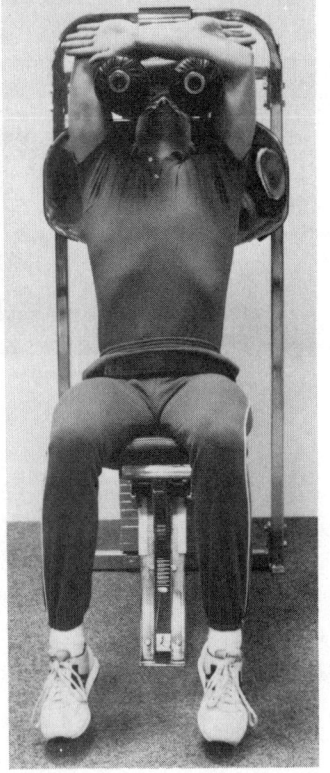

Bring arms overhead, pause for two, return. Palms still facing outward.

1. Set seat height so that the head rests fully on its pad.
2. Place arms under rollers and face palms forward.

SPORTSPERFORMANCE

40° CHEST/SHOULDER MACHINE

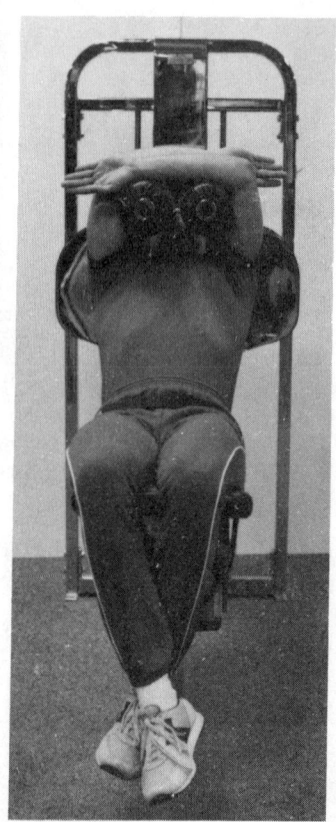

Finishing position.

Follow instructions as on 70° Shoulder Machine.

TORSO AND SHOULDERS

10° CHEST MACHINE

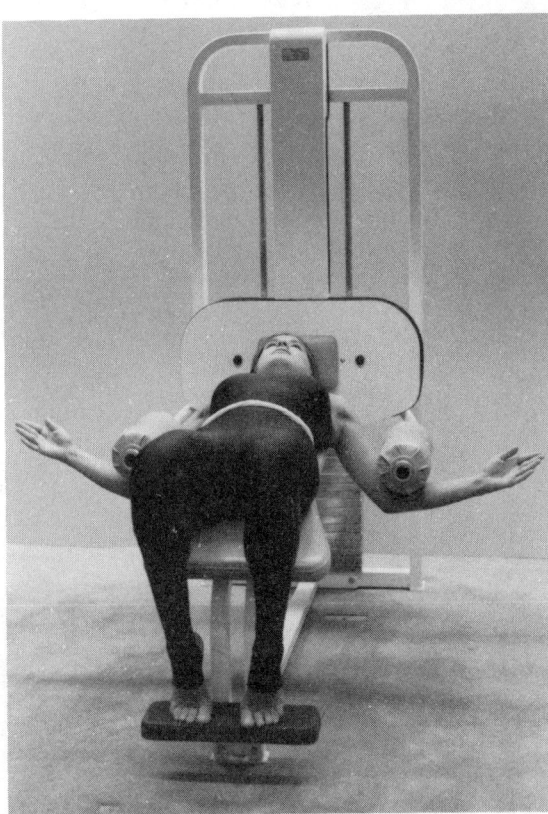

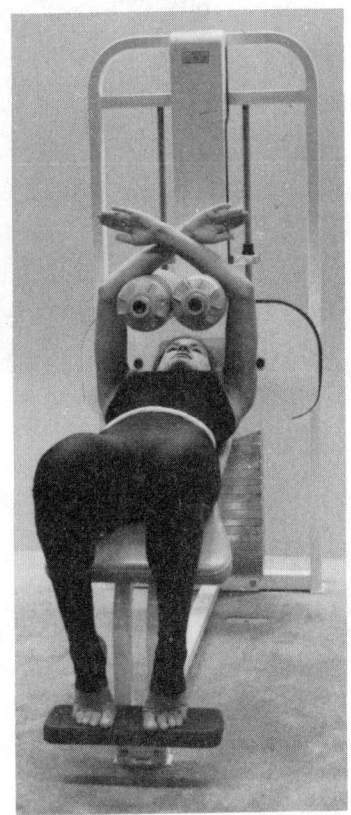

Contract then pause for a count of two overhead. Return and repeat.

Position body so that the upper arms form a 70°-90° angle with the torso. Palms face forward.

SPORTSPERFORMANCE

THE ROWING TORSO MACHINE

Sit against the front pad and place arms in front of rollers at a 90° angle to torso.

1. Slowly push backward as far as is comfortable. Hold in this position for a count of two then return slowly to starting position and repeat.
2. Remaining pressed into the front pad will help prevent you from arching your back as you contract.

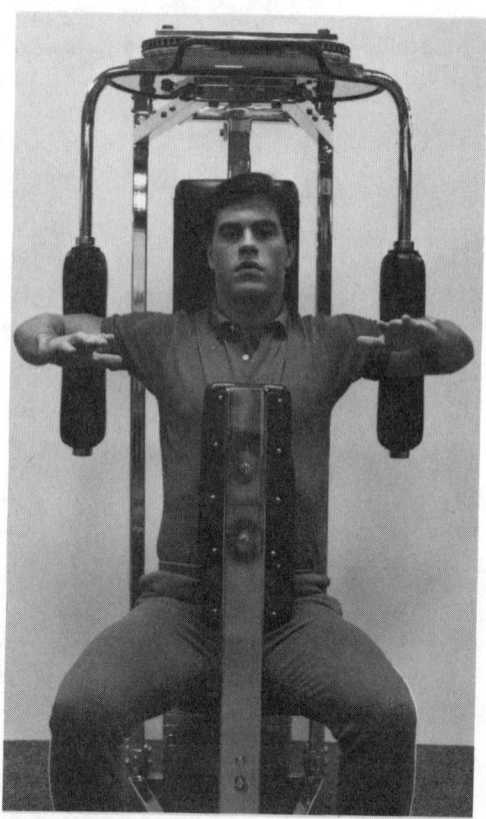

TORSO AND SHOULDERS

Alternate arm placement reduces stress on the shoulder joint. Starting position shown here.

Finishing position for reduced shoulder-stress variation.

SPORTSPERFORMANCE

THE FOUR-WAY NECK MACHINE

1. Anterior (front) Flexion: Set seat height so that your head makes full contact with the face pads.
2. Sit upright, grasp the crossbar with one hand and one handgrip with the other.
3. Let the head slowly extend backward by gradually reducing the assistance of the hand and assuming the load with the front neck muscles (in a negative or eccentric contraction). Place the second hand on the remaining handgrip.

1. From the fully extended position (head back), bring the head forward while keeping the torso completely motionless.
2. Pause in the contracted position then return slowly toward extension and repeat.

Lateral Flexion to the Right: Turn the body 90° and follow instructions as for front flexion.

1. *The torso again remains completely motionless and upright while the head flexes from side to side.*
2. *Turn 180° and work lateral flexion to the left.*

Posterior (rear) Flexion: Flex head front to back.

Keep the torso steady and the back straight while flexing and extending the head.

SPORTSPERFORMANCE

THE ROTARY NECK MACHINE

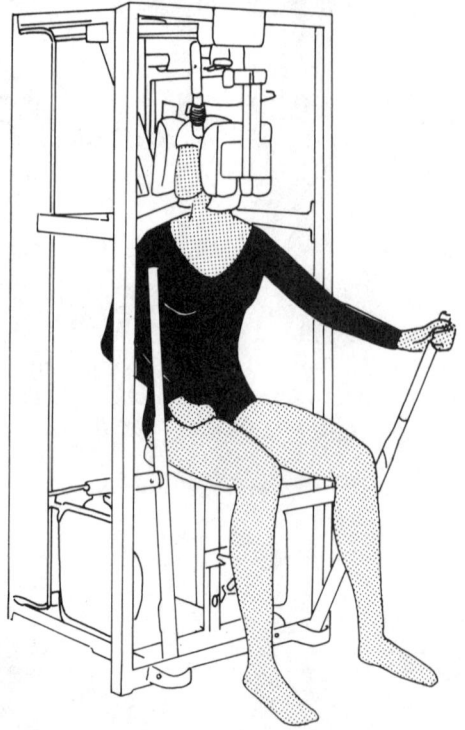

1. Get familiar with the lever that adjusts the head pads. You'll need to create a snug fit around your head to use this machine properly.
2. When you push the long, right-hand lever (to your side, that is) or pull the left lever, the head will be forced to rotate to the left. Your goal is to resist your arms (no weight stack here!) with the muscles that rotate the neck. Pushing the right-hand lever will therefore enable negative-only training of the neck rotator muscles that prevent rotation to the left.
3. Get familiar with the action of the two long levers before beginning a set.
4. Work one complete rotation from right to left and resist with your neck rotators.
5. Reverse your arm action and resist left-to-right rotation with your neck.
6. Do only six repetitions to each side.
7. Do not use this machine if you have a history of neck or upper back problems.

TORSO AND SHOULDERS

THE NECK AND SHOULDER MACHINE

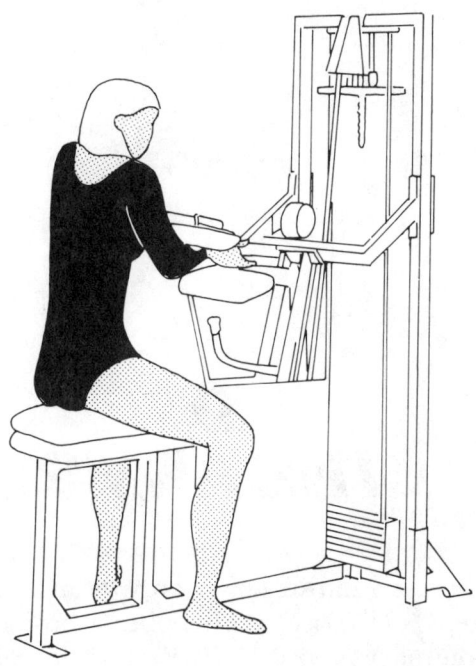

1. You are in the correct starting position when the weight load you have chosen is elevated off the weight stack with your shoulders down and relaxed. Most people will need to sit atop two or more pads to bring them to this starting height.
2. Arms are threaded between the forearm pads with palms facing up.
3. In the relaxed, shoulders-down position, remember that the weight stack you've chosen should be elevated.
4. Shrug your shoulders as high as possible, lifting the weight with the trapezius muscles and not the biceps. You may want to practice shoulder shrugs outside the machine first.
5. Hold in the elevated position for a count of two then return slowly and repeat.

9
THE ARMS

Your workout is winding down; only the arms remain. The Multi-Biceps and -Triceps units offer a host of variations, and the accurately named Multi-Exercise machine comes in quite handy as well.

Beginners should start with the simple bilateral curls (both arms working together). Next in the progression is unilateral training, where one arm either relaxes while the other completes a full rep, or holds isometrically in the *contracted* position while the other does a full rep. (These apply to the Multi-Triceps as well.) Other variations include: one-arm curls; one-arm, negative-only curls; isometrics; and infimetrics/akinetics. More on these variations follow below.

Muscle Groups	Nautilus® Machines

Elbow Flexors
  Brachialis, Biceps
  Brachii
	Multi-Biceps, Plateloading Biceps, Multi-Exercise Biceps Curls, Torso Arm, Multi-Exercise Chin-Ups, Multi-Exercise Upright Rowing

ARMS

Muscle Groups	Nautilus® Machines
Elbow Extensors	
Three heads of Triceps Brachii	Multi-Triceps, Plateloading Triceps, Exercise Triceps Extension, Multi-Exercise Dips, Overhead Press, Incline Press, Pullover
Wrist Flexors	
Flexor Carpi Radialis and Ulnaris	Multi-Exercise Wrist Curls
Wrist Extensors	
Extensor Carpi Radialis and Ulnaris	Multi-Exercise Reverse Wrist Curls

THE MULTI-BICEPS MACHINE

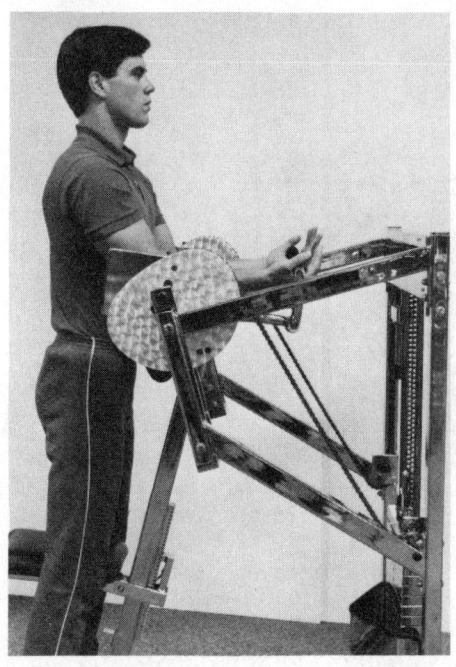

Grasp the handles before sitting down in machine. Note open-hand grip.

SPORTSPERFORMANCE

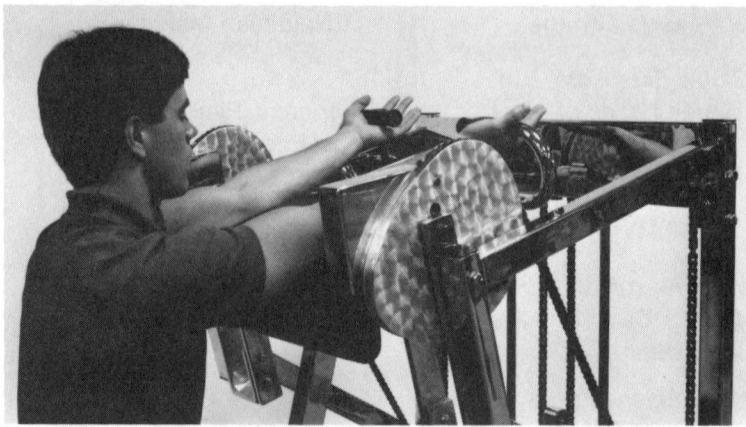

Set seat height so that a straight line drawn from the shoulder to the hands forms a 15°-20° angle with the floor. This is starting position. Shoulders are down (not shrugged), grip remains open.

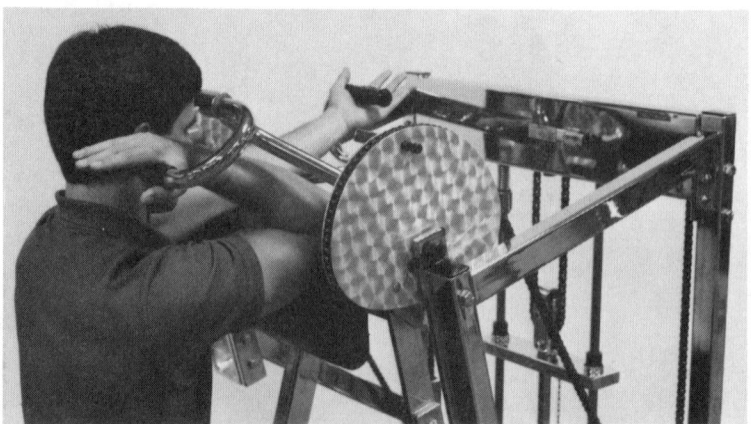

1. Both hands may be curled up to full flexion simultaneously (Curl 1, not shown), or one arm may remain extended while the other does a full rep (flexion then extension; Curl 2, shown).
2. For Curl 3, hold the flexed arm isometrically at the ear and do a complete rep with the other arm (extend then flex back to ear; same photo!).
3. Negative-only (Curl 4, not shown): Stand in machine, use two hands on one lever to bring it into the fully flexed position. Sit, then lower to a count of 10 with one arm only. Repeat up to 10 times, then switch to other arm.

1. Infimetric/Akinetic (Curls 5 and 6): Swing the infimetric bar into place above the weight stack (shown).
2. Pull on both levers simultaneously to bring the top plate (infimetric) or weight stack chosen (akinetic) up against the infimetric bar.
3. Begin curling one arm while resisting with the opposite arm. You will be doing a "concentric" or positive curl with the flexing arm and an "eccentric" or negative curl with the extending arm.
4. Keep the weights against the infimetric bar, taking five to ten seconds to complete one full curl with the flexing arm. Do not release tension and let the plate(s) drop off the infimetric bar.
5. Shoot for 10-12 curls with each arm.
6. For Curl 7: Isometric exercise can be performed with the infimetric bar in place. Since the arm that is extending eccentrically can create 30%-40% more force than the curling arm, it can prevent the curling arm from moving—hence an isometric contraction.
7. Begin with the right arm near full extension. Attempt to curl the right arm but hold it motionless with the eccentric contraction of the left arm. Hold a maximal contraction for about six seconds.
8. Move about one-third way through the curl then do another six-second isometric. Finish the exercise near full flexion, then repeat with left arm.

SPORTSPERFORMANCE

THE PLATELOADING BICEPS CURL

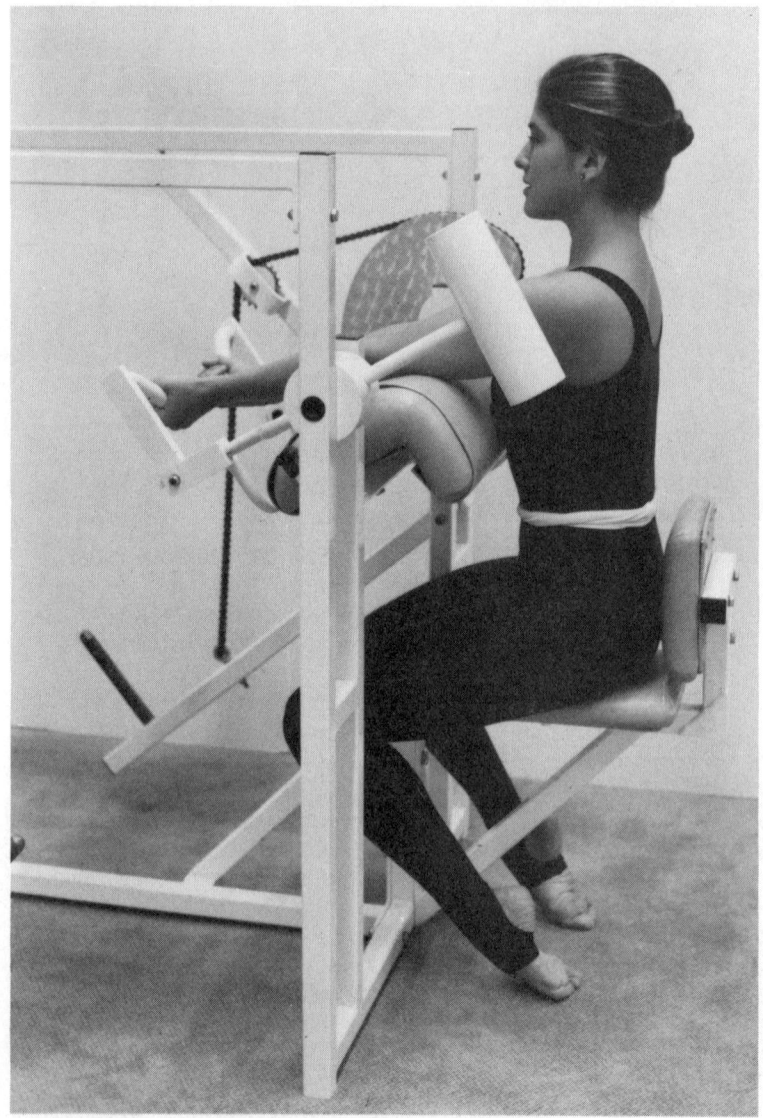

1. Sit upright, grasp rotating handlebar in the middle with the palms turned slightly inward.
2. Align elbow joint axis with the machine's axis of rotation.
3. Keep the shoulders down and relaxed (not shrugged).

ARMS

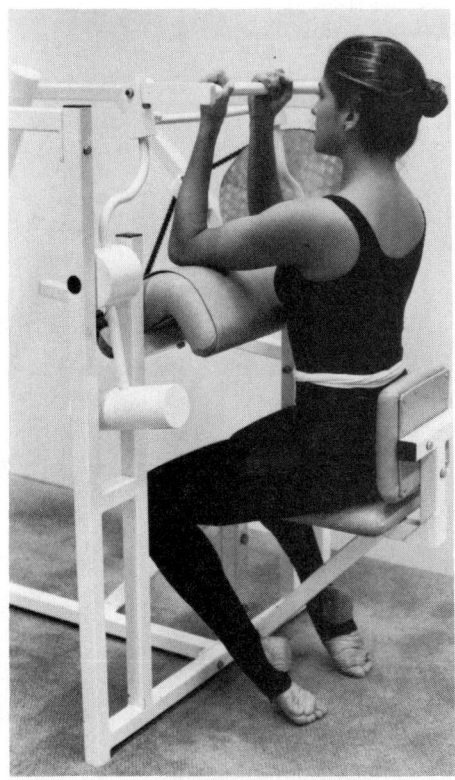

Curl slowly upward, using either a loose, closed grip or an open grip. Note good seated posture.

Finishing position. Elbows have maintained alignment with machine axis; posture is still good.

SPORTSPERFORMANCE

MULTI-EXERCISE MACHINE CURLS

1. Your range of motion won't be as complete on this machine, so use this exercise only when there's a long line to get to the Multi-Biceps or Plateloader.
2. Starting position. Good posture, elbows at side.

1. Finishing position. Greater range of motion can be obtained by letting the elbows swing slightly forward.
2. Hold in contracted position for a count of two, lower slowly, and repeat.

ARMS

MULTI-EXERCISE MACHINE UPRIGHT ROWING

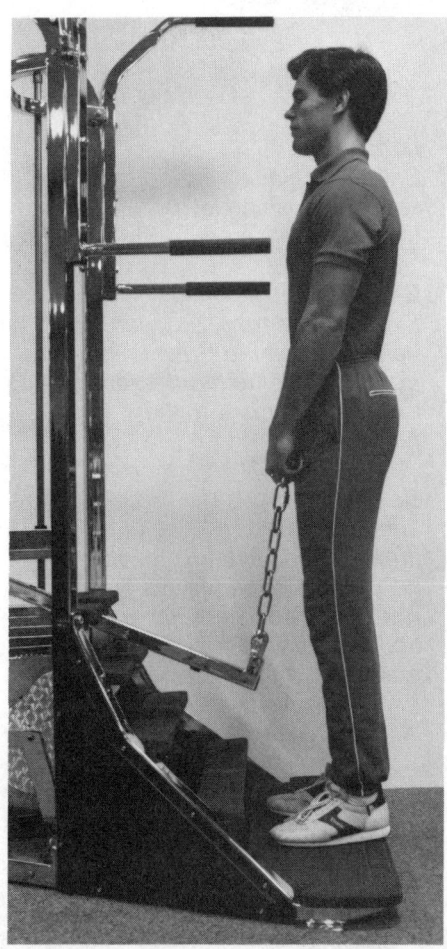

1. Pull upward slowly to chin, leading with elbows. Note flat back position.
2. Pause for two, lower slowly, and repeat.

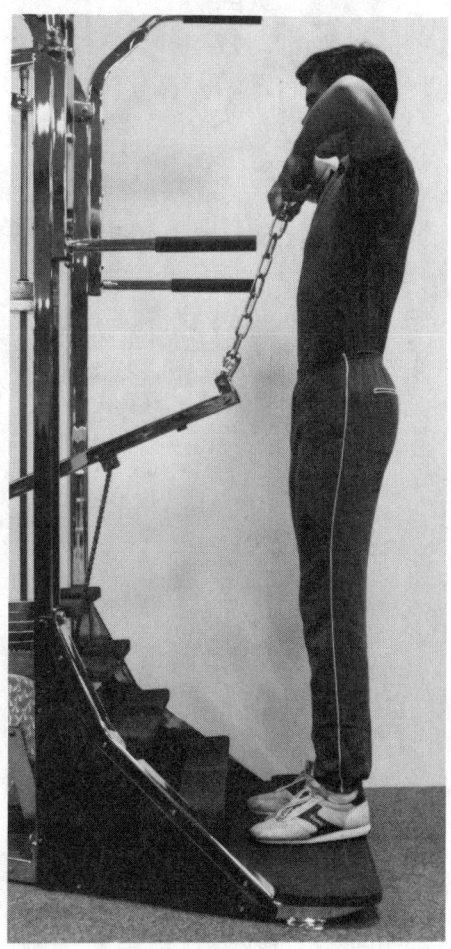

Same starting posture as left photo but reverse grip.

SPORTSPERFORMANCE

THE MULTI-TRICEPS MACHINE

Left:
Enter machine by straddling seat and pushing levers toward weight stack.

Below, left:
Extend both arms. Set seat height so that the straight line from shoulder to hand forms a 15°-20° angle with the floor.

Below, right:
Triceps Extension 1: Let both arms flex and extend simultaneously. Note hands in a "karate chop" position. Elbows are aligned with the center of machine rotation.

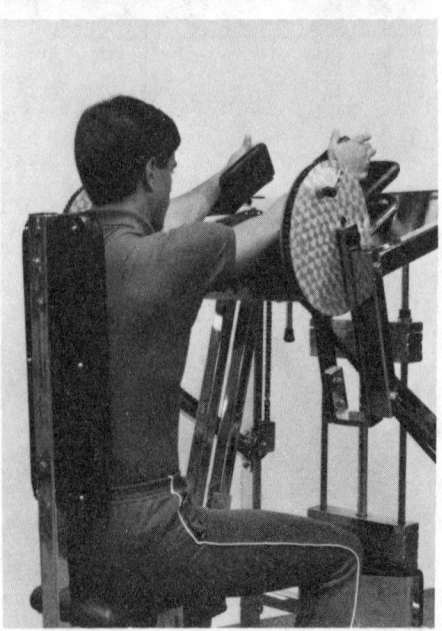

ARMS

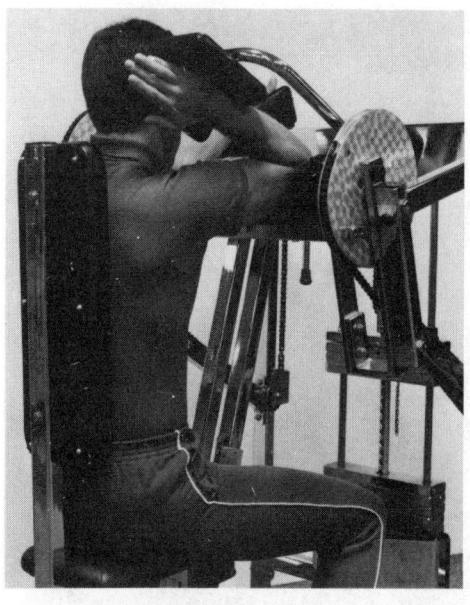

1. Triceps Extension 2: Hold one arm isometrically at the relaxed or flexed position and do a complete rep with the other arm (shown). Keep the shoulders down and relaxed.
2. Triceps Extension 3: Hold one arm isometrically in the extended (contracted) position, then do a complete rep with the other arm (same photo).

1. Infimetric/Akinetic (variations 4 and 5): Swing the infimetric bar into place above the weight stack.
2. Follow instructions as for the Multi-Biceps. One arm extends while the other resists. Do not let the top plate (infimetric) or plates (akinetic) drop off the infimetric bar.
3. Take 5–10 seconds to complete one flexion/extension; aim for 10–12 reps with each arm.
4. Isometric Extensions (variation 6): Follow instructions as for Multi-Biceps.

SPORTSPERFORMANCE

THE PLATELOADING TRICEPS MACHINE

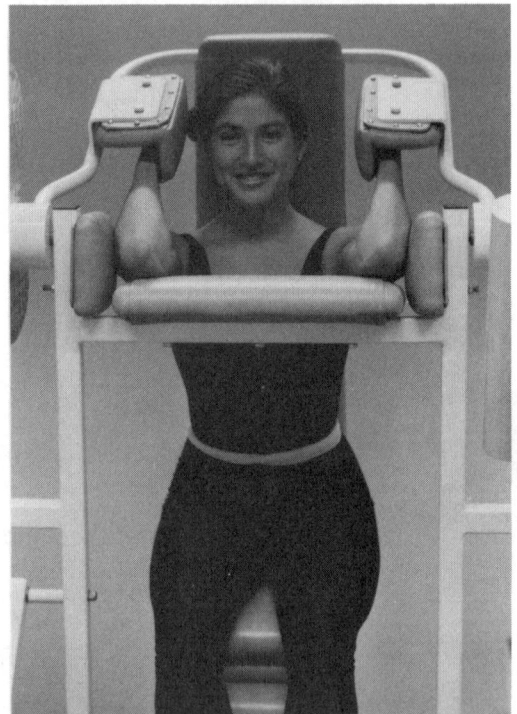

1. Straddle seat and enter as with Multi-Triceps. The shoulder to hand line should again form a 15°-20° angle with the floor. Use seat pads if the angle is much beyond 20°.
2. Let the machine draw you back into the flexed position.

1. Extend both arms simultaneously. Pause for two, return slowly, and repeat.
2. There is no correlation between the amount of weight you use on the Plateloader and the number of plates on the Multi-Triceps. You'll need to use trial and error to find your correct weight here.

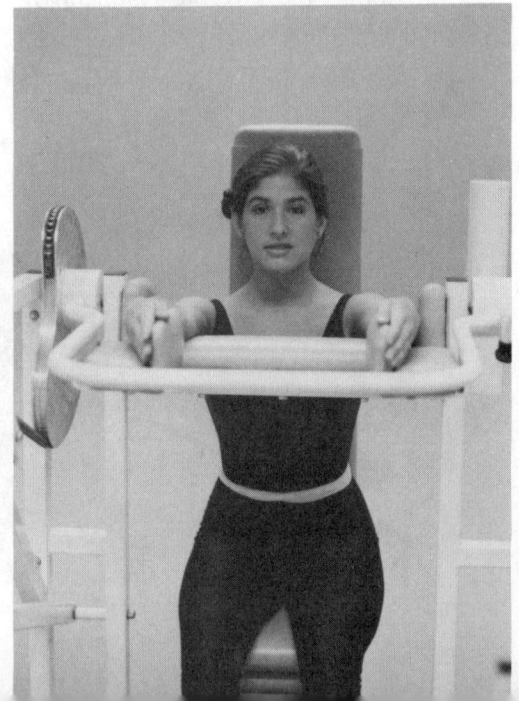

ARMS

THE MULTI-EXERCISE MACHINE TRICEPS EXTENSION

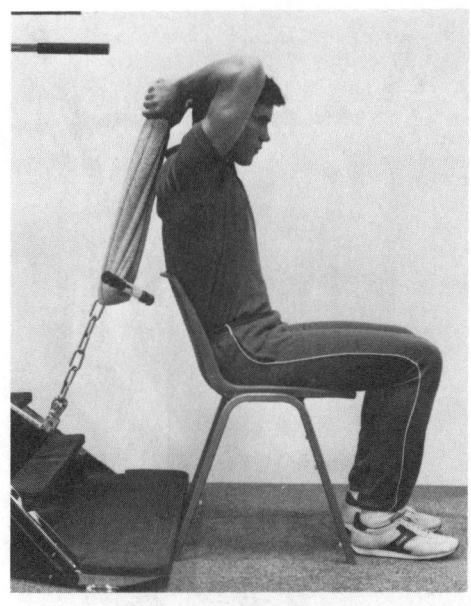

1. Find a sturdy chair and a long towel. Place chair against base of machine; run towel around chain and bar as shown.
2. Grasp securely with one hand on each end of the towel. Keep your back firmly planted in the chair. Position your arms so that the upper arms run alongside the ears.

Below:
1. Extend upward slowly keeping the elbows locked against the ears.
2. Hold in contracted position for a count of two, return slowly, and repeat.

SPORTSPERFORMANCE

MULTI-EXERCISE MACHINE TRICEPS DIPS

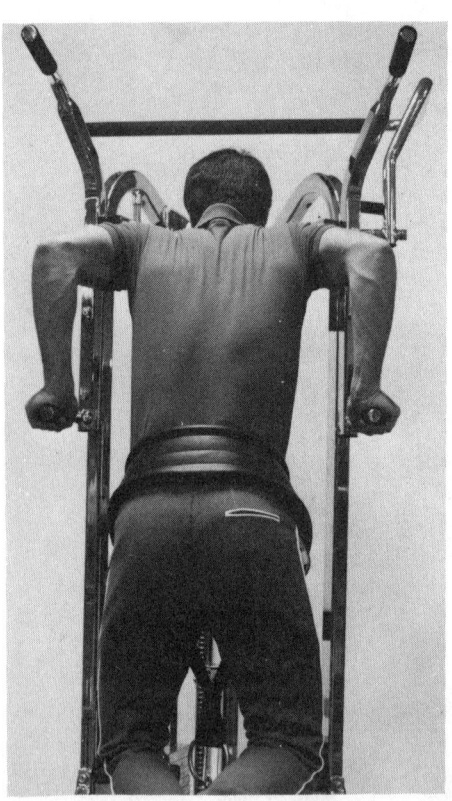 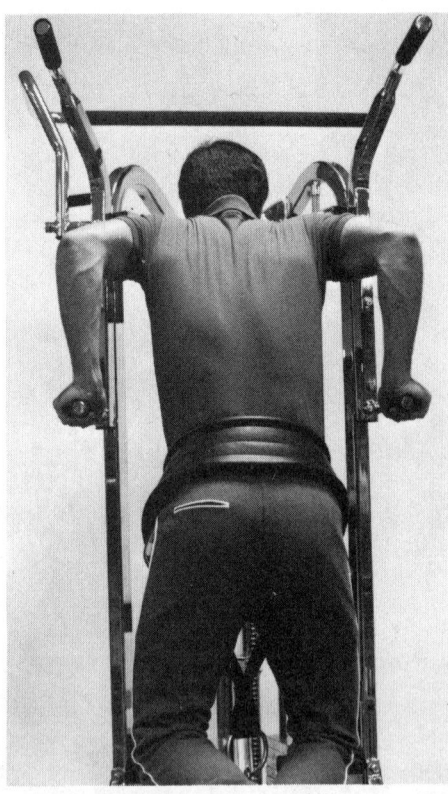

1. Starting position. The hip belt may be worn to increase difficulty if your body weight doesn't sufficiently challenge your triceps.
2. Flex knees and cross ankles.

Right:
1. Lower slowly until upper and lower arms form a 90° angle.
2. Press back up into starting position.
3. If you cannot do five complete dips, or wish to use negative-only dips for variety, lower yourself to a count of ten then climb back up the steps and repeat. Shoot for 10 negative-only reps, resting sufficiently between each to make this possible.

ARMS

MULTI-EXERCISE MACHINE WRIST CURLS

1. Position seat so that when bar is grasped, only the hands extend over the knees.
2. Start with the bar held by the fingers only. Keep your back as straight as possible, though some forward lean is required.

1. Begin by curling bar up with fingers.
2. Complete rep by closing grip and flexing hands as far as possible toward the forearms.
3. Pause for a count of two, lower slowly, and repeat.

SPORTSPERFORMANCE

MULTI-EXERCISE MACHINE REVERSE WRIST CURLS

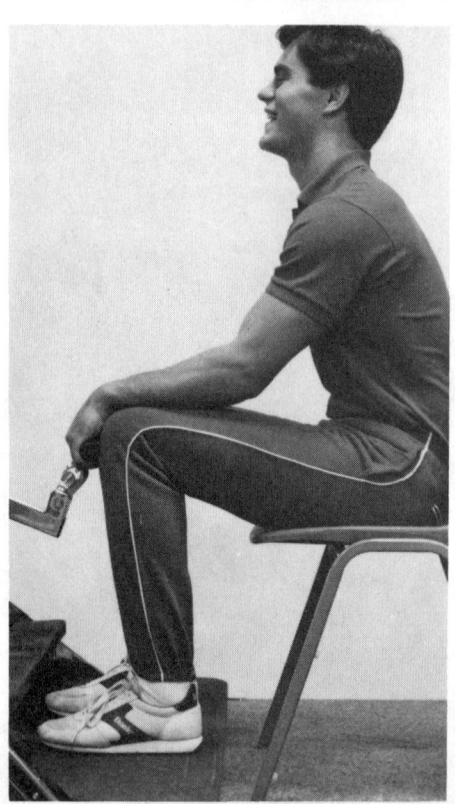

Use a reverse, palms-down grip. The fingers must obviously be closed in this exercise.

Curl upward as high as possible. Pause for two, lower slowly, and repeat.

10
28—COUNT 'EM—28 NAUTILUS WORKOUTS

Keep in mind that your workouts should be periodically changed to prevent staleness and plateaus, and refer every nine weeks or so to the 28 workouts that follow.

Although the first eight on the list are called "Beginner" workouts, they can be used by people at all levels of fitness. The "beginner" category is used simply to denote the absence of more advanced training options, such as negative-only, -emphasized, and -accentuated reps.

The seven "Mixed Workouts" combine standard positive-negative exercises with negative-type training. If you're a novice, you might experiment with these workouts after two or three months of standard training (Beginner workouts).

The five "Negative Workouts" are intended for the strong and Nautilus-experienced only. They *must* be done with a floor instructor or training partner, and with the express permission of the facility's owners/operators. Try one a week, at the most.

Finally, the five "Upper Body" and three "Lower Body" workouts are strictly for something wild and crazy to do every once in a while.

SPORTSPERFORMANCE

BEGINNER WORKOUTS

BEGINNER WORKOUT 1
1. Hip and Back
2. Leg Extension
3. Leg Press
4. Pullover
5. Torso Arm
6. Arm Cross (Double Chest)
7. Decline Press (Double Chest)
8. Lateral Raise (Double Shoulder or freestanding)
9. Overhead Press (Double Shoulder)
10. Biceps Curl (Multi-, Plateloader, or Multi-Exercise)
11. Multi-Exercise Wrist Curls
12. Multi-Exercise Reverse Wrist Curls
13. Abdominal

BEGINNER WORKOUT 2
1. Hip and Back
2. Leg Extension
3. Leg Curl
4. Behind Neck
5. Torso Arm
6. Rowing Torso
7. Multi-Exercise Triceps Dips
8. Biceps Curls (Multi-, Plateloader, or Multi-Exercise)
9. Multi-Exercise Wrist Curls
10. Multi-Exercise Reverse Wrist Curls
11. Multi-Exercise Calf Raises
12. Abdominal
13. Low Back

BEGINNER WORKOUT 3
1. Leg Extension
2. Duo Squat
3. Hip Adductor
4. Hip Abductor
5. Pullover

NAUTILUS WORKOUTS

6. Multi-Exercise Chin-Ups
7. Arm Cross
8. Decline Press
9. Biceps Curl (three machines)
10. Multi-Exercise Wrist Curls
11. Four-Way Neck (all four sides)
12. Abdominal

BEGINNER WORKOUT 4

1. Leg Extension
2. Duo Squat
3. Leg Curl
4. Behind Neck
5. Multi-Exercise Chin-Ups
6. Lateral Raise
7. Overhead Press
8. Rowing Torso
9. Biceps
10. Multi-Exercise Wrist Curls
11. Four-Way Neck
12. Multi-Exercise Calf Raises
13. Abdominal

BEGINNER WORKOUT 5

1. Hip and Back
2. Leg Extension
3. Leg Curl
4. Multi-Exercise Calf Raise
5. Foot Flexor on Leg Curl
6. Pullover
7. Behind Neck
8. 70° Shoulder
9. 40° Chest/Shoulder
10. 10° Chest
11. Biceps Curl
12. Triceps Extensions (Multi- or Plateloader)
13. Abdominal

SPORTSPERFORMANCE

BEGINNER WORKOUT 6
1. Duo Squat
2. Leg Curl
3. Multi-Exercise Calf Raise
4. Foot Flexor on Leg Curl
5. Pullover
6. Torso Arm
7. 70° Shoulder
8. Decline Press
9. Biceps Curl
10. Abdominal
11. Hip Flexor
12. Low Back

BEGINNER WORKOUT 7
1. Hip and Back
2. Duo Squat
3. Leg Curl
4. Hip Flexor
5. Adductor
6. Abductor
7. Multi-Exercise Chin-Ups
8. 70° Shoulder
9. Overhead Press (Double Shoulder)
10. Multi-Exercise Triceps Dips
11. Biceps Curl
12. Abdominal
13. Low Back

BEGINNER WORKOUT 8
1. Hip and Back
2. Leg Extension
3. Leg Curl
4. Adductor
5. Abductor
6. Pullover
7. Torso Arm
8. 70° Shoulder
9. 40° Chest/Shoulder

NAUTILUS WORKOUTS

10. Biceps Curl
11. Abdominal
12. Low Back

MIXED WORKOUTS

MIXED WORKOUT 1

1. Hip and Back
2. Leg Extension
3. Leg Press on Compound Leg
4. Adductor
5. Abductor
6. Pullover
7. Negative Multi-Exercise Chin-Ups
8. Arm Cross
9. Negative-only Decline Press
10. Multi-Exercise Triceps Dips
11. Negative-only Multi-Exercise Calf Raise (lift into raised position with help of arms; lower to a count of 10 with calves)
12. Abdominal
13. Low Back

MIXED WORKOUT 2

1. Pullover
2. Negative Multi-Exercise Chin-Ups
3. Lateral Raise
4. Rowing Torso
5. Negative-only Multi-Exercise Triceps Dips
6. Leg Extension—Negative-accentuated (lift with two legs, lower with one)
7. Leg Curl—Negative-emphasized (spotter applies extra resistance on the negative phase)
8. Multi-Exercise Calf Raise
9. Foot Flexor on Leg Curl
10. Abdominal
11. Hip Flexor
12. Low Back

SPORTSPERFORMANCE

MIXED WORKOUT 3

1. Duo Squat Akinetic (set your weight at 50%–75% of what you normally use; swing infimetric bar into place)
2. Leg Extension
3. Leg Curl
4. Adductor
5. Abductor
6. Pullover—Negative-only (use foot pedal or spotter to bring stack into contracted position)
7. Multi-Exercise Chin-Ups—Negative-only
8. 70° Shoulder
9. 40° Chest/Shoulder
10. Multi-Biceps Machine Curl—Negative-only (bring one lever into contracted position with two arms, lower with one)
11. Multi-Exercise Wrist Curls
12. Abdominal

MIXED WORKOUT 4

1. Duo Squat
2. Leg Extension—Negative-accentuated (raise with both legs, lower with one)
3. Leg Curl
4. Hip Flexor
5. Pullover
6. Negative-only Multi-Exercise Chin-Ups
7. Lateral Raise
8. Overhead Press
9. Negative-only Multi-Exercise Triceps Dips
10. Biceps Curls
11. Multi-Exercise Wrist Curls
12. Abdominal
13. Low Back

MIXED WORKOUT 5

1. Hip and Back
2. Duo Squat
3. Leg Extension—Negative-accentuated
4. Leg Curl—Negative-emphasized
5. Behind Neck

NAUTILUS WORKOUTS

6. Torso Arm—Negative-only (spotter brings bar down into contracted position)
7. 70° Shoulder
8. 10° Chest
9. Multi-Exercise Triceps Dips
10. Multi-Biceps Machine Curls—Negative-only
11. Abdominal
12. Rotary Torso
13. Low Back

MIXED WORKOUT 6

1. Hip and Back
2. Duo Squat
3. Leg Extension—Negative-emphasized (spotter applies resistance to foot rollers on negative phase)
4. Leg Curl—Negative-accentuated
5. Pullover
6. Multi-Exercise Chin-Ups—Negative-only
7. Lateral Raise
8. Overhead Press
9. Arm Cross
10. Decline Press—Negative-only
11. Multi-Triceps Machine—Infimetric
12. Multi-Biceps Machine—Infimetric
13. Abdominal

MIXED WORKOUT 7

1. Duo Squat—Infimetric
2. Leg Extension
3. Leg Curl
4. Adductor
5. Abductor
6. Behind Neck
7. Torso Arm—Negative-only (use spotter)
8. 70° Shoulder
9. Arm Cross
10. Multi-Triceps Machine—Infimetric (50% of normal weight load)
11. Abdominal
12. Rotary Torso
13. Low Back

SPORTSPERFORMANCE

NEGATIVE WORKOUTS

NEGATIVE WORKOUT 1
1. Leg Extension—Negative-accentuated
2. Leg Press (Compound Leg)—Negative-emphasized
3. Leg Curl—Negative-accentuated
4. Multi-Exercise Calf Raise—Negative-only
5. Pullover—Negative-only
6. Multi-Exercise Chin-Ups—Negative-only
7. Lateral Raise—Negative-only (use a spotter on each arm)
8. Overhead Press—Negative-only (use spotter behind machine)
9. Multi-Exercise Triceps Dips—Negative-only
10. Multi-Biceps Machine—Negative-accentuated
11. Abdominal—Negative-only (use spotter)

NEGATIVE WORKOUT 2
1. Hip and Back (normal)
2. Leg Extension—Negative-emphasized
3. Leg Press (Compound Leg)—Negative-emphasized
4. Leg Curl—Negative-only (use spotter)
5. Pullover—Negative-emphasized
6. Torso Arm—Negative-only (use spotter)
7. Overhead Press—Negative-only (use spotter)
8. Multi-Exercise Triceps Dips—Negative-emphasized (with hip belt)
9. Multi-Biceps Machine—Negative-only (one arm at a time)
10. Multi-Exercise Calf Raises—Negative-only
11. Abdominal—Negative-only

NEGATIVE WORKOUT 3
1. Pullover (normal)
2. Multi-Exercise Chin-Ups—Negative-emphasized (with hip belt)
3. Arm Cross—Negative-emphasized (spotter in front or one at each side)
4. Decline Press—Negative-emphasized (apply extra resistance against foot pedal)
5. 70° Shoulder (normal)

NAUTILUS WORKOUTS

6. Multi-Biceps Machine—Negative-only
7. Leg Extension—Negative-accentuated
8. Leg Curl—Negative-emphasized
9. Multi-Exercise Calf Raises—Negative-only
10. Abdominal (normal)
11. Low Back (normal)

NEGATIVE WORKOUT 4

1. Duo Squat (normal)
2. Leg Extension—Negative-emphasized
3. Leg Curl—Negative-accentuated
4. Multi-Exercise Calf Raise—Negative-only
5. Pullover—Negative-only
6. Multi-Exercise Chin-Ups—Negative-emphasized (with hip belt)
7. Overhead Press—Negative-only (with spotter)
8. Arm Cross (normal)
9. Decline Press—Negative-only
10. Multi-Exercise Triceps Dips—Negative-emphasized (with hip belt)
11. Multi-Exercise Machine—Upright Rowing (normal)
12. Abdominal
13. Low Back

NEGATIVE WORKOUT 5

1. Hip and Back (normal)
2. Leg Extension—Negative-emphasized
3. Leg Curl—Negative-emphasized
4. Multi-Exercise Calf Raises—Negative-only
5. Behind Neck (normal)
6. Multi-Exercise Chin-Ups—Negative-emphasized (with hip belt)
7. Arm Cross—Negative-emphasized (two spotters if possible)
8. Overhead Press—Negative-only
9. Multi-Exercise Triceps Dips—Negative-emphasized (with hip belt)
10. Multi-Biceps Machine—Negative-only (one arm at a time)
11. Abdominal
12. Rotary Torso

SPORTSPERFORMANCE

UPPER BODY WORKOUTS

UPPER BODY WORKOUT 1
1. Pullover
2. Torso Arm
3. Lateral Raise
4. Overhead Press
5. Arm Cross
6. Decline Press
7. Multi-Exercise Triceps Dips
8. Biceps Curl
9. Multi-Exercise Upright Rowing
10. Multi-Exercise Wrist Curl
11. Multi-Exercise Reverse Wrist Curl
12. Abdominal

UPPER BODY WORKOUT 2
1. Behind Neck
2. Torso Arm
3. 70° Shoulder
4. Rowing Torso
5. 10° Chest
6. Multi-Triceps Infimetric
7. Multi-Biceps Infimetric
8. Multi-Exercise Upright Rowing
9. Multi-Exercise Wrist Curls
10. Multi-Exercise Reverse Wrist Curls

UPPER BODY WORKOUT 3
1. Pullover
2. Multi-Exercise Chin-Ups
3. Lateral Raise
4. 70° Shoulder
5. Arm Cross
6. Decline Press
7. Triceps Extensions
8. Multi-Exercise Triceps Dips—Negative-only
9. Biceps Curl
10. Upright Rowing (Multi-Exercise)
11. Multi-Exercise Wrist Curls
12. Multi-Exercise Reverse Wrist Curls

NAUTILUS WORKOUTS

UPPER BODY WORKOUT 4
1. Pullover
2. Behind Neck
3. Multi-Exercise Chin-Ups—Negative-only
4. Lateral Raise
5. 70° Chest
6. Overhead Press
7. Arm Cross
8. Decline Press
9. Rowing Torso
10. Triceps Extensions
11. Biceps Curls
12. Abdominal

UPPER BODY WORKOUT 5
1. Behind Neck
2. Pullover
3. Arm Cross
4. Rowing Torso
5. Overhead Press
6. Multi-Exercise Triceps Dips
7. Multi-Exercise Upright Rowing
8. Biceps Curls
9. Multi-Exercise Wrist Curls
10. Multi-Exercise Reverse Wrist Curls
11. Abdominal
12. Low Back

LOWER BODY WORKOUTS

LOWER BODY WORKOUT 1
1. Duo Squat
2. Leg Extension
3. Leg Curl
4. Hip Flexor
5. Adductor
6. Abductor
7. Multi-Exercise Calf Raise
8. Foot Flexor on Leg Curl
9. Abdominal
10. Rotary Torso
11. Low Back

SPORTS PERFORMANCE

LOWER BODY WORKOUT 2
1. Hip and Back
2. Leg Extension
3. Duo Squat
4. Leg Curl
5. Adductor
6. Abductor
7. Multi-Exercise Calf Raise
8. Foot Flexor on Leg Curl
9. Abdominal
10. Hip Flexor
11. Low Back

LOWER BODY WORKOUT 3
1. Hip and Back
2. Duo Squat
3. Leg Curl
4. Leg Extension
5. Hip Flexor
6. Multi-Exercise Calf Raise
7. Foot Flexor on Leg Curl
8. Adductor
9. Abductor
10. Abdominal
11. Rotary Torso
12. Low Back

FINAL TRAINING NOTE

Advanced Nautilus users may find the following training method productive:

1. Get two weight-stack pins ready and a capable trainer to use them.
2. Place the first pin about three plates heavier than your usual training weight.
3. Place the second pin in the plate above the first.
4. Attempt three repetitions with perfect form at the unusually high starting weight. If you can't do this, start only two plates above normal.

NAUTILUS WORKOUTS

5. Have the spotter immediately pull the pin out of the bottom plate after the three reps and jump it over the second pin to the plate above that.
6. Attempt another three perfect reps with the weight that the second pin has set.
7. After these three reps, the trainer again jumps the pin upward and you start working with the weight that he or she set with the first pin.
8. Keep training as your spotter jumps the pins upward and over each other to the first plate—if you can last that long! Don't use this technique more than twice a workout—it's brutal.

11
WHERE TO WORK OUT

Before joining a new center, or renewing a current membership, it's in your best interest to reread the section in Chapter 2 on credentials, then return here for information on choosing the best fitness center for your money.

Should you decide that your hectic schedule limits your three weekly visits to the fitness center to 30 minutes each, and you want to purchase some home equipment to fill the void, the chapter closes with recommendations for the best in home fitness.

FINDING QUALITY IN COMMERCIAL FITNESS CENTERS

Long the places to go for whirlpool, steam, sauna, and massage, "health spas" have increasingly metamorphosed into "fitness centers," those high-tech palaces for body reshaping, making the job of getting the most from your dollars harder and harder.

Unfortunately, many fitness entrepreneurs staff their facilities with young, hard bodies who may be long on fitness but short on fitness *acumen*. Faced with machines using

WHERE TO WORK OUT

compressed air, water, hydraulics, and weight plates, and bikes, rowers, skiers, treadmills, and climbers bristling with electronics, how can you safely and effectively become fit? Here are some suggestions on how to find the best fitness center for your money.

With time and creeping boredom being the two most often-cited reasons people become fitness dropouts, the two things you need to look for first in a fitness center are *proximity to home and/or job* and *wide selection of fitness equipment and programs.* No matter how good your original intentions, a long commute to and from the fitness center will eventually become a powerful reason to quit. Few choices of aerobic and strength equipment, or unvarying and uninteresting classes, may also bring a quick end to your fitness dreams. Top fitness facilities will offer all or most of the equipment and classes listed below. By all means, bring this book with you on your next visit.

EQUIPMENT AND PROGRAM GUIDE

STRENGTH EQUIPMENT

Machines: Look for Nautilus, Eagle by Cybex, Cam II, Polaris. Smaller centers may offer multistation Universal Gym equipment.

Free weight: Look for a wide selection of Olympic bars; fixed-weight bars; dumbbells, curl-bars; and flat, incline, and decline benches.

AEROBIC EQUIPMENT

Treadmills: A club should sport at least three units, having no less than 1.5-horsepower motors. Treadmills with elevation let you train at walking speeds but with high caloric expenditure levels (no need for the high-impact forces of running). Better manufacturers are Marquette, Quinton, Trotter, Landice, Pacer, and Precor.

Stationary bikes: De rigueur at better clubs are computerized bikes that take you up and down hills and compute your ever-improving aerobic fitness levels. Look for Lifecycles, Biocycles, and Heartmates, and in sufficient numbers

SPORTSPERFORMANCE

to accommodate their popularity! Not as much fun but certainly as effective at burning calories all over and training your lower body are nonelectronic bikes by Monark and Bodyguard. These latter bikes *must* be the commercial grade—weighing 100 pounds or more—in order to survive.

Rowing machines: Hydraulic rowers (using automobile-like shock absorbers) by Precor, Proform, and Avita are tops in their class. Much closer to actual rowing, and often more fun, are rowing simulators by Concept II and AMF. The latter unit offers fingertip selection of 20 electronic levels of working resistance, caloric expenditure, and elapsed time.

Ski simulators: Cross-country simulators by the two reputable competitors NordicTrack (PSI) and Fitness Master offer excellent aerobic benefits with none of the impact forces of running. Look-alike but low-quality units are being rushed to market, so stick with the leaders.

Climbing devices: Look for the Stairmaster, a compact miniescalator that brings the aerobic and leg-shaping benefits of stairclimbing outside the stairwell. For more advanced users, the VersaClimber, an eight-foot climbing stalk that simulates ladder climbing with variable hydraulic intensity, is a top equipment choice.

Minitrampolines: Also called rebounders, these devices have been found to be of limited utility to the already fit. If you're significantly overweight or a fitness novice, though, these can get you off on the right track.

AEROBIC FACILITIES

Running track: Indoor tracks that are so short that they require more than 12 laps to the mile may put excessive wear and tear on your ankles, knees, and hips from the constant turning. You're better off on a treadmill.

Swimming pool: A scandal bigger than Watergate: An Olympic-size pool has only one length—exactly 50 meters (55 yards), or 165 feet. If one more fly-by-night health spa advertises their useless 40-foot pool as Olympic-size, there may be violence! Seriously, expect only minimal fitness benefits from a pool that's less than 20 yards long—or else you'll be turning at a wall every few seconds.

WHERE TO WORK OUT

Racquetball/squash: If you are at least moderately skilled, and matched with the right opponent (someone of equal or slightly greater ability), these activities do offer aerobic benefit. But not if your rallies last a shot or two, and are followed by a significant amount of gabbing. Tennis is rarely considered on an aerobic par with running/swimming/cycling/rowing/skiing.

CHOREOGRAPHED CLASSES

Aerobic dance: While there are easy-to-follow rules for assessing equipment and facilities, there is no easy way to determine the safety and efficacy of choreographed classes. You can't be too cautious, because the vast majority of classes are either unsafe, not aerobic, or both. You'll need to inquire about the various instructors' credentials (schooling, certification programs or seminars attended, etc.), and view at least two classes, to make an intelligent decision. A good class will contain these components:

- A gentle warm-up lasting at least 10 minutes, which will include easy stretching and whole-body movements that accelerate in pace and intensity over the period. If you see any moves even faintly resembling a standing or bouncing toe touch, *leave.*
- An aerobic segment of at least 20 minutes. To be truly aerobic, the movements must make rhythmic and repetitive use of the large muscles of the legs and buttocks for the entire 20 minutes. Frequent pauses to allow pulse measurement are a must in beginner classes.
- An optional calisthenic segment for strength and abdominal work. Many centers now devote entire classes to such maneuvers.
- A cool-down of at least *10 minutes,* including light stretching and continued gentle, whole-body movements. Again, standing toe-touch moves are definitely o-u-t.

A good general rule, especially valuable when checking out classes, is to visit a fitness center at the time of day you're likely to use it. A 2:00 P.M. class may be small and well supervised, but if you're going to work out with 60 others at 6:00 P.M. on a dance floor fit for 30, forget it.

And speaking of dance floors, the dancing surface has a major effect on injury rates. Better fitness centers are springing for (excuse the pun) high-tech floors that cushion landings without decreasing the stability of the foot on landing. Avoid at all costs the carpet-on-concrete floors so frequently found in women-only spas with never-ending two-for-one or $99-a-year membership offers.

MISCELLANEOUS PROGRAMMING

You may find yoga, martial arts, stretching-only, and calisthenics-only classes in the bigger and better fitness centers. Once again, classes are only as good as those who lead them. Find out as much as you can about the instructors, and watch at least one class before joining.

FITNESS TESTING

A service that should be considered an important, almost-absolute prerequisite to joining a center is fitness assessment. A trained staff member (preferably an exercise physiologist) should conduct painless, safe, and not-terribly-time-consuming tests of your aerobic condition, muscular strength, and flexibility. The results will enable the staff member to write you an "exercise prescription," an exact plan that tells you which equipment to use or classes to take, and for how long, how often, and how hard.

TRAINING AT HOME

PENNY WISE, POUNDS SMART

High technology has entered the realm of home exercise equipment, making it possible for fitness buffs to consider the home as a private fitness center. With annual membership dues at the more serious commercial exercise centers ranging from $400 to $1,000-plus, it makes sense to look into a one-time expenditure that will provide five years or more of safe, effective exercise for the entire family. The home fitness center also eliminates a major reason for avoiding exercise: lack of time.

WHERE TO WORK OUT

Will an investment in home equipment replace "professionally supervised" exercise? Yes. For that $400-$1,000, a family can purchase two to four pieces of equipment and one or more first-rate books on home exercise—and never miss the fitness center. Whether it uses aerobic exercise for weight control and cardiovascular benefits, or strength training to shape the body or train for recreational sports, the new generation of home equipment is safe, relatively easy to use, and best of all, highly effective. You may miss the motivational charge that comes with group exercise. If you are one who would miss getting a boost from 30 other sweating bodies, you may want to keep your health club membership active.

LOW-BUDGET HOME FITNESS

You can meet your cardiovascular and strength needs on a surprisingly low budget. Walking, jogging, and running require little more than a good pair of running shoes, for which you should expect to spend a minimum of $40. Don't skimp on good running shoes, which are found nationwide at chain stores specializing in athletic footwear. When considering those $19.95 specials at your local discount store, remember that an office visit to an orthopedist or sports podiatrist may cost $100 or more.

To augment a gradual and progressive walk/jog/run program, you might consider buying hand-held weights. Most popular are Heavy Hands by AMF American—a starter set of one-pound, padded-grip weights costs $14-$20. As your fitness level climbs, additional pairs of weights can be added for $10-$15. Early research supports the concept that swinging hand-held weights brings more muscle into action, increasing aerobic benefits and burning additional calories. Ankle weights, or weighted vests, are for more advanced participants who need additional training challenges. Triangle Health and Fitness Systems offers a similar program of wrist and ankle weights, starting at $12.99 and increasing with the user's capacity to handle more poundage.

For exceptional strength-building or leg-toning benefits,

SPORTSPERFORMANCE

try a progressive program of stair climbing or hill running. With proper instruction from a trainer or exercise physiologist, you can get most or all of the benefits of expensive fitness center weight machines. Not for the unfit or those without fitness savvy, stairs and hills are a terrific "home" exercise option at no charge.

IS HOME FITNESS FOR YOU?

Though accurate figures are not yet available, a large proportion of the 1986's billion-dollar home-equipment sales is most likely gathering dist. Truthful, carefully considered answers to the following questions will help you decide which equipment is right for you.

- What financial commitment can you make to home equipment? How much can you spend now, and how much are you willing to spend to complement your initial purchase? As you'll see, you can find "best buys" if you look for them, but expect to spend no less than $200 for a stationary bike or rower, and $350-plus for home strength-training machines.
- How much space do you have available for home equipment? Golden rule number one of home fitness is "out of sight, out of mind." Once you store that bike or rower in a closet, it will most likely remain there. If you must use a closet, be sure to buy equipment that rolls or is easily carried.
- Are you and your family members candidates for self-supervised exercise? Discuss this with the family doctor, because home exercise can pose hazards for those with medical or weight problems. With a doctor's guidance, careful use of available literature, and helpful tools such as pulse monitors, people will benefit from exercise at home.
- What are the needs of those who will be using the equipment? If weight control and/or cardiovascular health are the primary needs, you'll want to stress aerobic equipment, such as the stationary bike and rowing machine. If users are already aerobically fit from outside pursuits such as running or swimming,

WHERE TO WORK OUT

but need strength and muscle for recreational or cosmetic purposes, strength equipment should be the first acquisition.
- Do you really think you'll use the equipment? Being honest with yourself now will save a great deal of money if your answer is no. A renewed commitment to exercise, though, may be just what the doctor ordered. Perhaps investing in a bike, rather than in a $2,000 six-piece gym, would be a good way to test your new resolve. Are you a socially motivated exerciser, who needs group-stimulated adrenaline to keep at it? If that is the case, stick to the spa.

THE SHOPPING LIST

Answers to prepurchase questions in hand, you're ready to consider the following choices in home equipment:

AEROBIC TRAINING DEVICES

- Stationary bicycles
- Rowing machines
- Cross-country skiing simulators
- Treadmills
- Minitrampolines (rebounders)
- Jump ropes

STRENGTH TRAINING DEVICES

- Barbells
- Dumbbells
- Multipurpose gyms
- Portable "gyms"

DUAL PURPOSE
(Aerobic and Strength)

- Pulse monitors
- Hand-held weights
- Ankle Weights

SPORTSPERFORMANCE

For upper-body strengthening, two old standbys still offer top results. Push-ups build chest, upper-arm, shoulder, and back strength. Chin-ups, on a door-mounted bar (various manufacturers, about $12.95), build the complementary muscles not trained with push-ups. Combine the two and just about every muscle from the waist up can be trained—for less than $15.

AEROBIC EQUIPMENT

Stationary bicycles. The single most popular piece of home equipment, the stationary bike offers aerobic, weight control, and leg shaping benefits without the jarring impact of jogging or running. While it doesn't provide as efficient a workout for the entire body as ski simulators or rowers, a bike is a fine first acquisition for the home.

At about $200, the Tunturi Home Cycle is the least expensive recommended bike. The Tunturi sports a friction mechanism, a nylon strap around a heavy flywheel, used by the better home bikes. This device lets you smoothly increase pedaling intensity to speed calorie burn and leg toning. The Tunturi's seat and handlebars are easily

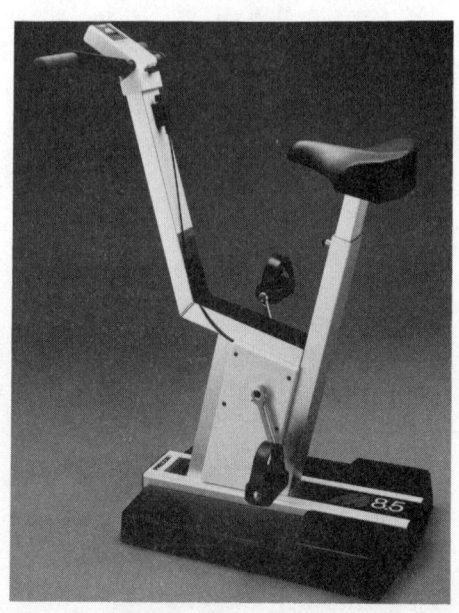

The Precor M8.5. Top-notch riding—uses a horizontally spinning flywheel and unique transmission. About $800. (Photo courtesy of Precor, Inc.)

The Bodyguard 955 Ergocycle. Felt by many to be the best buy in the $300 range. (Photo courtesy of J. Oglaend, Inc.)

The Precor 820e. A smooth and silent belt-driven bike. (Photo courtesy of Precor, Inc.)

adjustable, allowing a custom fit for all family members.

In the $300 to $400 range, stationary bikes by Bodyguard and Monark offer smoother rides, better adjustability, and greater comfort. These prices may sound steep, but remember that the more comfortable you are on the bike, the more likely you'll be to use it. These bikes also offer gauges that give feedback on pedaling intensity or workload, making day-to-day increases easy to administer.

In the $550 to $700 range are excellent bikes by Paramount, Schwinn, and Precor. Paramount's "The Chair" is a "recumbent" design that places you comfortably in a seated and reclined position, with the pedals out in front rather than below. You select and control your workload electronically, via LED displays of time and calories burned. The advantages of recumbent cycling? Physiologically, it appears that you'll burn more calories at the same or even easier workloads. Practically, you're no longer perched precariously on a narrow and uncomfortable seat. Your bottom, and, more important, your back are fully supported. With these boosts in comfort and safety, you're more likely to keep coming back for more.

The Schwinn Airdyne's unique mechanism combines a standard pedaling arrangement with handlebars that can be pushed and pulled in a rowing motion. You may use them separately or with the pedals, and the spinning fan blades, instead of a flywheel, provide the resistance, keeping you cool while you work out.

The Precor 830e uses a horizontal flywheel that spins like a record platter. Through a direct drive mechanism, it yields a smooth-as-silk ride even at high pedaling workloads. A full spate of electronic information rounds out the Precor's feature list.

For about $1,400, Bally Fitness Products Corporation offers the Home Lifecycle, a computerized marvel that takes you up and down hills by increasing and decreasing pedaling intensity in an almost infinite variety of patterns. The Lifecycle has spawned several competitors, which now offer integral color TVs or FM radios with headphones. Prices for these deluxe entries have climbed past $3,000.

Rowing machines. Requiring coordinated action of the legs, buttocks, back, and arms, rowing is a more complete, more demanding exercise than stationary cycling, and it is not a wise first purchase for the unfit. What makes a good rowing machine? Precision of fit in the moving parts is number one in importance, and this quality begins to show up in machines selling for $200 and up. Look for tightness of fit in all bearings and moving or rolling parts. The seat must be comfortable and move freely, and the shock-absorber-like pistons should offer smooth, even resistance through the full range of motion. As a general rule, rowing machines claiming to do 10 different things and costing less than $200 usually fail to do any of them well.

WHERE TO WORK OUT

The Precor M6.2. One of the premier hydraulic-piston rowers. (Photo courtesy of Precor, Inc.)

Topping the list of inexpensive, high-quality rowers is the West Bend 5100, a dual-piston machine with tight-fitting parts, that retails for about $200. Rowers in the $260 to $380 range include those from Precor, Proform, and Avita. All offer ultra-high quality and the right features. Let local price discounts and your personal fit in the machine help you decide among these.

AMF American's Benchmark 920 rower (about $600) is a seven-foot electronic version of the excellent but much longer Concept II rower (about $650). Both forgo the hydraulic pistons of the lower-priced models for a single oar-and-flywheel mechanism. An automobile alternator provides computer-controlled resistance in AMF's rower, while a cast aluminum wheel with wind vanes provides the resistance in the Concept II. If you can afford the steeper cost, and have the room, these rowers offer a superb simulation of the actual rowing experience. The Benchmark rower scores higher on many experts' scorecards because of its electronic control over the 20 levels of resistance, and LED readout of time and caloric expenditure. The Concept II, however, offers a more realistic rowing simulation.

The Avita 970 Precedence Series. A quality piston-type rower with resistance in both directions. (Photo courtesy of M&R Industries, Inc.)

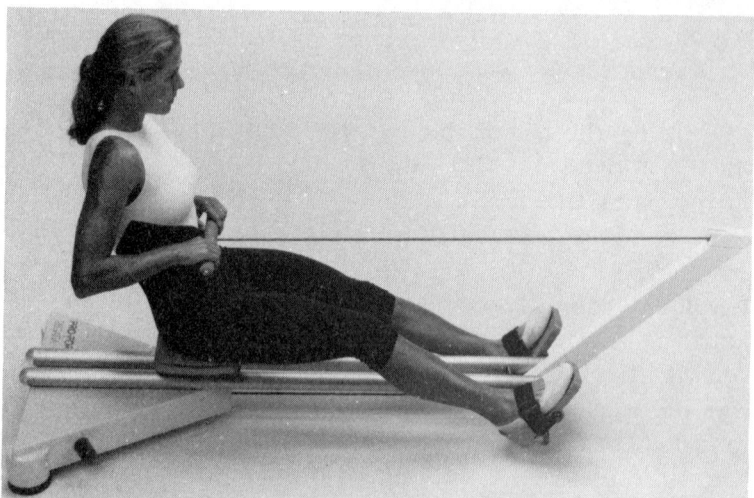

The Pro-Form Regatta. Latest in the center-pull rower category. Folds for easy storage. (Photo courtesy of Pro-Form, Inc.)

Cross-country skiing simulators. Like rowing machines, these devices challenge both upper- and lower-body muscles, providing cardiovascular conditioning without the impact on the joints incurred during running. Best known is the NordicTrack skier by PSI (about $600). The Nordic-Track is thought by some to offer a more realistic simulation of the poling and striding action of cross-country skiing

The Fitness Master LT-35. A zero-impact, whole-body workout for under $400. Independent adjustment of arm and leg tension. (Photo courtesy of Fitness Master, Inc.)

The Fitness Master SnoBound'r. Just introduced, this Alpine (downhill) ski simulator is a twist on the minitrampoline. (Photo courtesy of Fitness Master, Inc.)

than its competitors, since the wooden skis are not fully fixed in their tracks. The Fitness Master LT-35 ($399) and XC-1 ($529) are excellent choices, however, provide more balanced leg development, and are far easier to learn.

Treadmills. If you must run, but prefer to do it in the more pleasant environment of your home, treadmills are an expensive but effective option. Few nonmotorized treadmills offer a smooth-enough surface to keep you running over the long haul. The Avita 350 motorized but nonelectronic treadmill (about $1,100) has a hefty 1.5-horsepower motor and a top speed of 10 mph, and is roughly half the price of fine but expensive models from Precor that come with and without elevation ($2,200 to $2,800).

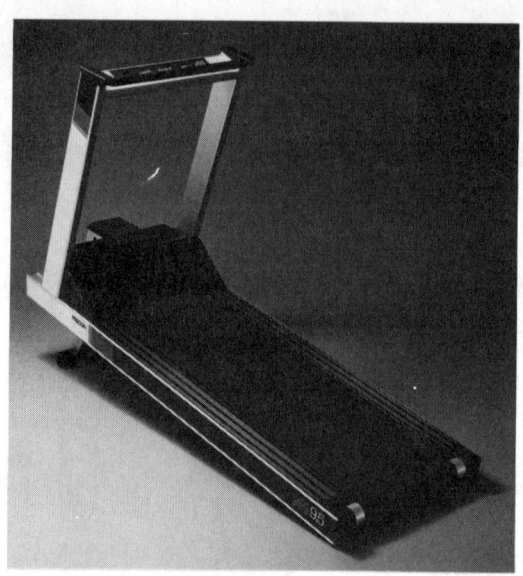

The Precor M9.5. A state-of-the-art electronic treadmill. (Photo courtesy of Precor, Inc.)

Minitrampolines. Often called rebounders, these are an inexpensive aerobic alternative that provide sufficient intensity for aerobic conditioning. You'll spend between $50 and $100. Experts suggest that square or rectangular models are likely to be easier on your feet and ankles. The connection between frame, springs, and trampoline bed should be as secure as possible.

Jump ropes. Given healthy feet, ankles, and knees, jumping rope is an inexpensive yet highly aerobic training option. Skip the long-handled jump ropes (about $30), which tend to fall short of advertised promises, and go with either the less-than-$10 versions, or try a new item called Heavy Rope (about $30), which comes in weights from 1.5 to 6 pounds, and uses sand to fill a hollow, one-inch diameter rubber rope. Swung more slowly than a regular rope it offers some unusual upper-body strength benefits.

STRENGTH TRAINING EQUIPMENT

Barbells and dumbbells. Available everywhere, these low-tech, little-ticket tools still build muscle. Sometimes called "free weights," they come in various forms: dumbbells are hand-held and can hold up to 40 pounds in most home sets. Standard barbell sets, with a single, five-foot steel bar, usually hold a maximum of 135 pounds. Few home gyms need both dumbbells and barbells, but if several family members will be working out simultaneously, it

The Precor 720 Incline Trainer. An ingenious device that uses body weight as the resistance. Changing body position changes the exercise. (Photo courtesy of Precor, Inc.)

might be wise to buy both. With an adjustable bench that allows seated and supine presses ($100–$300), a complete weight set for the family can be had for as little as $200, though plastic- or rubber-coated weights and sturdier benches can raise that figure. For more advanced trainees, "Olympic" weight sets, with more massive bars and weights, run in the $300-plus range.

Multipurpose gyms. From elastic cords for $39.95 to chromed-weight-stack units that can run $8,000, there's a wide and confusing selection of home strength training options. The class of the field in each price category are as follows:

- Less than $100. Used carefully, the elastic-cord system called the Lifeline Gym (about $40) can substitute for more elaborate devices. Practical for travel and spur-of-the-moment exercise.
- About $500. Far and away the top choice is Precor's Model 720 Incline Trainer. A novel design that uses your body weight as the source of resistance, the 720

offers at least 70 safe and effective exercises requiring no adjustments to the machine. Due to its cable-and-pulley system, the 720 adapts to your body's movements, while its more costly weight-stack-type competitors force you to adapt to the machine's limited range of movement. Weight-stack units in the under-$500 range generally should be avoided, because of poor manufacturing tolerances.

- $500 to $1,000. Marcy offers several models with heavy weight stacks and high-quality construction. The popular Soloflex unit (about $700) and its many spin-offs require time-consuming configuration changes each time you switch exercises. If a space-consuming weight-stack unit is not for you, choose the less expensive Precor 720 over the Soloflex and its $600 to $800 competitors.

- $1,000 and up. Look to Universal and Paramount for top-of-the-line, multipurpose weight-stack units. If your basement has at least 300 square feet of space, the Paramount 12-station Fitness Trainer, in beautiful chrome for about $8,000, is the ultimate home gym acquisition. After 15 years of dominance in commercial fitness centers, Nautilus Sports/Medical Industries, Inc. has scaled down its equipment for the home market. Since these single-function Nautilus machines each cost about $500, a complete home strength setup might exceed $3,000.

PULSE MONITORS

Tying it all together is the pulse monitor, a device that offers instantaneous and critical feedback on your body's response to exercise. Most frequently used to guide training intensity during aerobic work—where your pulse should fall within an age-adjusted "target zone" for maximum benefit—the monitor also can keep you within safe limits during strength work.

Why not simply take your pulse manually? Convenience and accuracy are the two main reasons, since you won't need to interrupt your workout periodically, and you won't

The Nautilus Home Rotary Torso machine. So effective they modeled the new commercial unit after it. (Photo by Marti Cohen-Wolf)

miscount 10 beats or more in the heat of action.

Many pulse monitors ($29 to $150) that use fingertip or earlobe sensors are terribly sensitive to the high forces found in running and vigorous rowing; they may be used with confidence only on stationary bikes. While chest strap models ($150 to $300) are a bit more cumbersome, they are highly accurate. Look for units that let you set high and low alarms, notifying you when you stray from your heart-rate target zone.

Technology at its finest is seen in CIC's "Uniq" pulse monitor ($329). A wireless system broadcasts your heart rate from a miniature chest strap transmitter to a microcomputer on your wrist. Besides sporting high-low alarm and stopwatch functions, the Uniq can store your heart rate response for up to 4 hours of exercise (at 5- or 15-second intervals), and play it back for analysis. All the rage in elite athlete circles, the Uniq is an extraordinary addition to anyone's fitness program.

A final word: Don't buy exercise equipment without having each family member likely to use the device test it. Carefully considered purchases will give you years of safe fun and fitness!

12
THE LATEST FROM NAUTILUS

I have seen the future of Nautilus and it looks grand! The four newest machines shown on the pages that follow should have found their way into fitness centers by the time you read this—and if not, ask for them. By incorporating several new, significant design features, they put Nautilus right back into position as a strength training technology leader.

Where other manufacturers had briefly gotten the jump on Nautilus was in the elimination of friction from machine operation. The four new Nautilus machines incorporate a low-friction design, using roller bearings, improved bushings, improved weight-stack guide rods, and prelubricated, higher-quality chain. You'll feel the difference on your first rep.

Less obvious to you as a Nautilus user, but of almost equal importance, is the addition to the weight-stack chain of a "slack adjuster," which will let management tighten up the chain as the machine wears in. (Most weight-stack machines require that links be removed to reduce slack, and it's rare to see management actually take the time and trouble to do it.)

LATEST FROM NAUTILUS

THE NEW MACHINES

THE ROTARY TORSO MACHINE

The Nautilus Home Rotary Torso machine was so good they reengineered the commercial model to duplicate and enhance it. By locking your arms in place and rotating your torso, you get an excellent training effect on the internal and external obliques and transverse abdominus—the muscles that, cosmetically speaking, serve a girdlelike function across your midsection.

THE COMPOUND ROWING MACHINE

Totally new for Nautilus is this rowing-type machine, which trains the latissimus dorsi of the midback, teres groups of the upper back, deep scapular muscles, back deltoids, and biceps and brachialis of the front of the upper arm. This machine will be excellent either on its own, replacing the Pullover or Behind Neck machines, or as an *adjunct* to either of them, being used immediately afterward in a latissimus preexhaustion routine.

THE TORSO ARM MACHINE

Similar to the Compound Rowing machine in that it works the middle and upper deck, and biceps and brachialis of the upper arm, the improved Torso Arm machine is not so much a radical change from the older version as it is a low-friction and biomechanical enhancement. Use it in your workout routines just as you would the old Torso Arm.

THE BENCH PRESS

Though more and more experts agree that the bench press has been overrated and overused as a measure of strength and/or power, it's still a favorite among those who train for strength, and an excellent way to build the pectoralis group and triceps. The new low-friction Nautilus Bench Press, like the Compound Rower, will be great on its own (use it to replace the Arm Cross for variety), or as a terrific second machine in a preexhaustion routine for the pectoralis (replace the Decline Press of the Double Chest with the Bench Press).

SPORTSPERFORMANCE

USING THE NEW MACHINES

THE ROTARY TORSO

In this, its first generation, the Rotary Torso seat has only two positions: 45 degrees left and 45 degrees right. It's likely that future generations of this machine will offer a wider range of adjustments to accommodate the differences in range of motion among users.

Sit erect in the seat with your head beneath the pivot point above you. Lock your arms over the rollers and keep your elbows tucked in tight.

From the forward-facing starting position, rotate your torso slowly and as far as possible in the direction of your knees, hold briefly, then return. Think "abdominals," keep your back pressed firmly against the carriage, and don't let the arms do any independent work.

After completing a set to the first side, pull back on the seat handle, rotate to the opposite side, and relock the handle. Work one more set to this side and you're on your way to a tight torso.

THE COMPOUND ROWING MACHINE

Seat height on the new Compound Rower should be set so that, when holding the handles (for most readers the *lower* handles), the arms are parallel to the floor or angled slightly downward. Sitting and remaining forward with your chest against the chest pad, pull slowly backward as far as is comfortably possible. Hold briefly, return slowly, and repeat to set completion.

THE TORSO ARM MACHINE

Set seat height so that the handles overhead are just within reach. The seat belt is especially important in this machine, so cinch it tight. Holding the handles on the inside, straight portion with a firm but not overly tight grip, lean forward, then pull. Keeping the elbows back, bring the hands down to shoulder height. Hold briefly then return slowly, still leaning forward, getting a good stretch at the top. If you're unable to extend fully, lower the seat one notch. If a staff member or training partner is nearby, you

Rotary Torso Machine.

Compound Rowing Machine.

Torso Arm Machine.

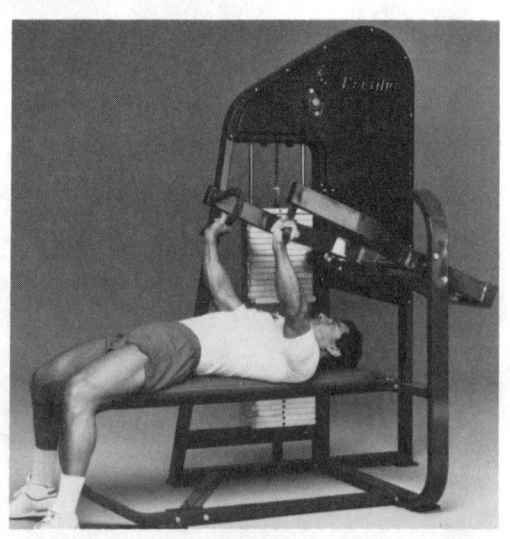

Bench Press.

can ensure a good stretch by lowering the seat so that the bar must be handed to you. Repeat to set completion.

THE BENCH PRESS

Lie flat on the bench with the handles in the mid-to-upper-chest area. With an open grip, press slowly upward to just short of lockout. Hold briefly, lower to starting position, and repeat to set completion.

INDEX

Abdomen
  workouts for, *illus.* 75–81
Abdominal machine, *illus.* 75–77
Abductor machine, *illus.* 71
Active rest, 41
Adductor machine, *illus.* 70
Aerobic capacity, 43
Aerobic dance, 29, 31, 145
Aerobic dance certification, 7
Aerobic equipment, 143, 150–56.
  See also Equipment
Aerobic exercise, 2, 8, 14, 27, 33
  benefits of, 29–30
  def. of, 28–29
  health benefits of, 34
  low-stress, 12
  time needed for, 28, 29
Aerobic facilities, 144–45
Aerobic power, 40
Aerobic training, 11–15, 34
  devices for, 149
Aerobics and Fitness Association
  of America, 7
American College of Sports
  Medicine, 7

Anaerobic power events, 41
Ankle weights, 147, 149
Appetite, 35
Arms
  workouts for, *illus.* 114–28
Athletes, 50
  professional, 44

Barbells, 26, 46, 149, 156–57
Basal metabolic rate, 30
Behind neck/torso arm machine,
  illus. 88–91
Bench press machine, 3, 161
  use of, 164
Bicycles
  stationary, 11–12, 143–44, 149,
    150–52
Biomechanics, 6
Blood
  pooling of, 33
Body composition, 17–18
  measurement of, 1
Body fat, 1
  reduction of, 14, 27, 29, 43
  stored, 29, 35

Body temperature
  cycle of, 14
Bodybuilders, 44
Bodylink, 22-23
Bodylog, Inc., 23
Books, 5, 28
Boredom, 11, 34, 37
Breakfast
  vs. dinner, 15
Breathing, 54
  heavy, 11

Calisthenics, 10
Caloric intake, 30
Calories
  correct allotment of, 16
Cams, 46
Cardiovascular system, 33
Chin-ups, 150
Chronobiology, 14
Circuit weight training, 29
Classes
  calisthenics-only, 146
  choreographed, 145-46
  stretching-only, 146
Climbing devices, 144
Climbing simulators, 31
Compound leg machine, *illus.* 67
Compound machines, 50, 53
Compound rowing machine, 3, 161
  use of, 162
Concentric contraction
  def., 21-22
Concentric-concentric exercise, 22
Conditioning
  combining strength and aerobic, 27-43
Continuous training, 37
Contractions
  muscular, 20
Cool-downs, 34, 36, 37
Coronary artery disease, 16
Coronary incidents, 27, 33, 54
Coronary risk, 49
Credentials, 6
Cross-country skiing simulators, 149, 154-55

Cross-training
  for nontriathletes, 13
Cybex Eagle, 24, 44
Cycles
  work/rest, 41
Cycling, 13, 28, 33, 37
  outdoor, 12, 29
  stationary, 28, 31

Degenerative conditions, 27
Diabetes, 49
Dieticians, 8
Digestion
  effects on metabolism, 14
Dinner
  vs. breakfast, 15
Doctors, 36
Double chest machine, *illus.* 96-100
Double shoulder machine, *illus.* 101-103
Dual purpose devices, 149
Dumbbells, 149, 156-57
Duo squat machine, *illus.* 62-64
Duration of exercise
  determining, 33-35

Eat to Win, 6
Eating, 15-17
Eccentric contraction
  def. of, 22
Effective load, 46
Eicosapentanoic acid, 16
Electrical impedance, 17
Electronic feedback, 12
Endurance, 2
Energy, 52
  high vs. low, 14
Enzymes, 20
Equipment, 2, 39, 143-44
  home, 31, 36
Exercise
  alternating with rest, 35
  before/after eating, 14
  positive-negative vs. negative-negative, 22
  psychology of, 6
  vs. rest periods, 37

INDEX

Exercise consciousness, 44
Exercise duration, 37
   definition of, 39-41
Exercise intensity, 37, 39
Exercise physiologist, 7
Exercise plans
   writing of, 30-36
Exercise science, 10
Exercise types, 39
Exertion
   perceived, 33, 39
Experts, 6-7

Failure, 53
   momentary, 47, 48, 49
Fainting, 54
Fartlek training, 42
Fat
   loss of, 17
Fats
   polyunsaturated vs.
      monounsaturated, 16
Fitness, 2, 5-18
Fitness centers, 3, 11, 36, 52, 142-43
Fitness gain, 11
Fitness level climbs, 147
Fitness Master, 12, 31
Fitness testing, 146
40° chest/shoulder machine, *illus.* 106
Four-way neck machine, *illus.* 110-11
Free weights, 10, 24, 143
Frequency of exercise
   determination of, 35
Frequency of repetitions, 41-42

Genetics, 10
Goals, 20
Gyms, 26
   multipurpose, 157-58
   portable, 149

Health, 2, 5, 27, 29
Heart disease, 11, 49
Heart rate, 53
   age-adjusted, 11

   elevated, 28
   high, 11
Heart rate response, 39, 40
   measurement of, 31-32
Heavy Hands, 147
Hip and back machine, *illus.* 59-61
Hip flexor machine, *illus.* 74
Hormones, 29
   fat-mobilizing, 34
   male, 10
Hutchins, Ken, 9, 52
HydraFitness, 22
Hydrostatic weighing, 18
Hypertensive, 49

Ice skating, 28
Illness, 27
Impact trauma, 12
Inactive rest, 41
Injuries, 13, 35
   overtraining-induced, 35
   reducing the risk of, 52
Intensity of exercise
   determining, 31-33
   measurement of, 31-33
   minimum required, 11
International Dance-Exercise Association, 7
Interval training, 34-35, 36-42
Interval training prescriptions, 36
Ironman triathletes, 13
Isokinetic contraction
   def. of, 23
Isometric contraction, 22-23
Isotonic contraction
   def. of, 23

Jogging, 14, 28, 147
Joint movements
   excessive, 12
Jones, Arthur, 2, 45, 47
Jump ropes, 149, 156

Keiser Company, 26
Keiser machines, 44

Ladder climbing, 28

SPORTSPERFORMANCE

Lasting the duration, 34-35
Lateral raise machine, *illus.* 104
Leg curl machine, *illus.* 68-69
Leg extension machine, 9, *illus.* 65-66
Lethargy, 35
Lifestyle, 49
Lower back
   workouts for, 58-74, *illus.* 75-81
Lower back machine, *illus.* 80-81
Lowering phase, 54

Machines, 2, 10, 36, 143
   cam-type, 23
   compound. *See* Compound machines
   variable-resistance, 23
Marathons, 13
Martial arts, 146
Maximum overload, 51
Meals
   vs. snacks, 15
Measurement, 6
Metabolism, 14
Milking, 33
Minitrampolines, 144, 149, 156
Momentary failure, 47, 48, 49, 53.
   See also Failure
Motor learning, 6
Multi-biceps machine, 9, *illus.* 115-17
Multi-exercise machine
   calf raise, *illus.* 72
   chin-ups, *illus.* 94-95
   curls, *illus.* 120
   foot flexor, *illus.* 73
   reverse wrist curls, *illus.* 128
   triceps dips, *illus.* 126
   triceps extension, *illus.* 125
   upright rowing, *illus.* 121
   wrist curls, *illus.* 127
Multi-triceps machine, *illus.* 122-23
Multipurpose gyms, 149
Muscles
   force output of, 23
   loss of, 17
   overloading of, 45
   overstressing, 43

pliability of, 52
range of motion, 45
sculptured, 8
skeletal, 8
well-defined, 27
Muscular endurance
   def. of, 20-21
Muscular failure, 48

Nautilus
   the latest from, 160
Nautilus Sports/Medical Industries, Inc., 24, 44
Nautilus training
   history of, 44-45
   rules for, 53-54
Neck and shoulder machine, *illus.* 113
Negative contraction
   def. of, 22
Negative phase, 54
Nonathletes
   training cycles for, 11
NordicTrack, 12, 31
Nutrition, 1, 5-18

Obesity, 49
Overtraining, 35

Performance
   quality athletic, 2
Performance levels, 39
Physical education, 6
Physiology, 14
Plateloading biceps curl machine, *illus.* 118-19
Plateloading triceps machine, *illus.* 124
Positive contraction
   def. of, 21
Power, 2
   def. of, 21
   development of, 25-26
Power events, 41
Precor, Inc., 12
Precor Simulator, 31
Preexhaustion principle, 47
Pullover machine, *illus.* 83-86

INDEX

Pullover/torso arm machine, *illus.* 87
Pulse monitors, 31–32, 149, 158–59
Push-ups, 150

Racquet sports, 29
Racquetball courts, 145
Reading, 30
Rebounders, 29
Records
  keeping of, 54
Recovery, 37
Relaxing, 30
Repetitions, 48
  number of, 49–51
Resistance, 46
Rest, 41
  active, 41
  inactive, 41
Rest periods
  vs. exercising, 37
Resting heart rate, 35
Roller-skating, 28
Rope jumping, 28, 31, 41
Rotary neck machine, *illus.* 112
Rotary torso machine, 3, 161, *illus.* 78–79
  use of, 162
Rowing, 28, 31, 34
  lake/river, 12
Rowing machines, 12, 144, 149, 152–53
Rowing torso machine, *illus.* 108–109
Runners, 40
Running, 12, 13, 28, 33, 37, 147
Running tracks, 144

Schedules
  planning of, 36
Scientists, 29
Sets, 48–49
  negative-only, 51
  number of, 48
  vs. repetitions, 47
70° shoulder machine, *illus.* 105
Shoulders
  workouts for, 82–113

Simulators, 11–13
Ski simulators, 144
Ski-tuning, 12
Skiing
  alpine, 12
  cross-country, 12, 31, 53
  nordic, 28
Skinfold pinch measurements, 17, 18
Sleep
  quality of, 35
Snacks
  vs. meals, 15
Snobound'r, 12
Sokol, Steve, 20
Soma-Tech, 18
Speed
  between machines, 51–52
Speedplay. *See* Fartlek training
Sprinting, 40
Squash courts, 145
Stair climbing, 28, 34
Stairmaster, 12
Stationary bikes. *See* Bicycles, stationary
Strength, 8, 19–20
  attainment of, 24–25
  maximum, 45
  science of, 2, 19–26
Strength curves, 24
Strength machines, 11
Strength research, 24
Strength training, 42
  high intensity, 21
Strength training equipment, 143, 149, 156–58. *See also* Equipment
Stress, 49
Stroke, 54
Super circuit, 52
Sweating
  heavy, 11
Swimmers, 40
Swimming, 13, 29
Swimming on the clock, 40
Swimming pools, 144–45

Target heart-rate zone, 32–33, 36, 53

Target-zone aerobics, 34
Target-zone training, 34
Temperatures
    internal, 52
10° chest machine, *illus.* 107
Tendons
    pliability of, 52
Testing, 6
Torso
    workouts for, 82–113
Torso arm machine, 3, 161, *illus.* 92–93
    use of, 162
Training, 2, 40
    at home, 146–59
    balanced, 2
    combining aerobic with
        strength, 42–43
    cyclical, 10–11
    differences, 8–9
    Fartlek. *See* Fartlek training
    lower body, 12
    male vs. female, 10
    quality vs. quantity, 8
    specificity of, 20
    speed of, 51
    speed-specific, 25
    upper body, 12
Training cycles, 11
Training intensity, 48–49, 52
Training notes, 140–41
Treadmills, 12, 37, 40, 143, 149, 155
Tri-Tech, 12
Triathlons, 13
Type of exercise
    determining, 30–31

Ultrasound, 17

U.S. Merchant Marine Academy, 42

Variable resistance training, 45–47
    def. of, 24
    correct, 46
Versaclimber, 13
Videotapes, 5, 28

Walking, 28, 31, 33, 53, 147
Warm-ups, 34, 36, 37, 52
Weight control, 29, 33
Weight loss, 11
Weight machines
    pulley-type, 46
Weight rooms, 26
Weighted vests, 147
Weights
    hand-held, 147, 149
    moving, 54
Women, 10
Work
    def. of, 21
Work/rest cycles, 41
Working out
    when to schedule, 13–14
Workload, 39
Workouts, 36, 43, 129–41
    beginner, 130–33
    frequency of, 36, 52
    lower body, 139–40
    mixed, 133–35
    negative, 136–37
    negative-only, 51
    upper body, 138–39
    varying of, 10–11

Yoga, 146